THE COMPLETE
ILLUSTRATED
GUIDEBOOK TO

BOSTON'S
PUBLIC
PARKS
AND
GARDENS

Concept, Design, and Maps by
Richard J. Berenson

Text by Jon Marcus

Photography by Susan Cole Kelly

Produced for
Silver Lining Books
New York
by
Berenson Design & Books, Ltd.
New York

SILVER
LINING
BOOKS

NEW YORK

For information address:
Silver Lining Books, 122 Fifth Avenue, New York, NY 10011

Library of Congress Cataloging-in-Publication Data is available on request.

ISBN 0-7607-2757-0

First Edition

Additional credits:

Photographic Archives of the Arnold Arboretum: *97, 98–99 bottom*
Copyrighted by the President and Fellows of Harvard College
Harvard University, Cambridge, Massachusetts, USA

Ballou's Pictorial Drawing Room Companion, **Dec. 3, 1859:** *33 top*

Boston Park Commission Report, 1883: *52*

Boston Public Library, Print Dept.: *74-75*

© CORBIS: *125 middle*

© CORBIS/Bettman: *20, 21 bottom, 42 top right*

© Kevin Fleming/CORBIS: *45 right*

© Lee Snider; Lee Snider/CORBIS: *31*

© Gary M. Blazon:
    83 top right, 84 bottom right, 86 top, 88 left, 89 bottom left

© Howard Friedman: *70–71 (fish illustrations)*

Library of Congress, Washington, DC:
    *11, 16-17, 25 bottom, 34-35, 46-47 bottom, 53,
    76-77 bottom, 78 bottom*

Norman B. Leventhal Map Collection: *21 top*

**Courtesy of the National Park Service,
Frederick Law Olmsted National Historic Site:**
    61, 142-143, 144 middle and bottom, 146-147, 151

© Picture Research Consultants & Archive: *32–33 bottom*

Zoo New England: *80, 81 bottom (© Sonja Rodrique)*

This book is dedicated to
Frederick Law Olmsted for his inspired vision
and to the staff and volunteers
of the
Boston Parks Commission,
the Emerald Necklace Conservancy,
and the Arnold Arboretum.

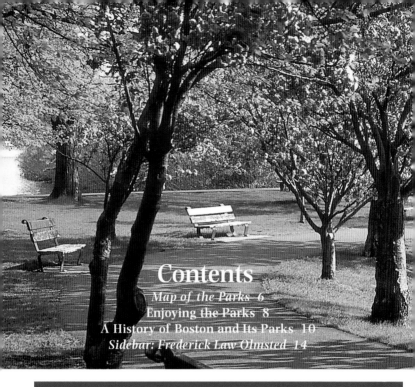

Contents

Map of the Parks 6
Enjoying the Parks 8
A History of Boston and Its Parks 10
Sidebar: Frederick Law Olmsted 14

THE EMERALD NECKLACE

BEYOND THE NECKLACE

ACKNOWLEDGMENTS
The authors wish to thank the following people and organizations for their invaluable assistance:
The Boston Parks Commission and Commissioner Justine Liff; the Metropolitan District Commission;
the staff of the Arnold Arboretum; Forest Hills Cemetery and the Forest Hills Educational Trust;
the Emerald Necklace Conservancy and Director Simone Auster; the Boston Harbor Islands National
Recreation Area; the National Park Service and the staff of the Frederic Law Olmsted National
Historic Site; Jack Fleming and the Boston Athletic Association; Zoo New England and Hugh Dolly;
and the Friends of the Public Garden.
An array of articles, publications, and books were also mined for information.
But a special debt is owed to the following authors and their works:
Ida Hay, *Science in the Pleasure Ground: A History of the Arnold Arboretum* (Northeastern University
Press, 1995); Witold Rybczynski, *A Clearing in the Distance* (HarperCollins, 1999); S. B. Sutton, *Charles
Sprague Sargent and the Arnold Arboretum* (Harvard University Press, 1970); Cynthia Zaitzevsky,
Frederick Law Olmsted and the Boston Park System (Belknap Press/ Harvard University Press, 1983);
The Public Garden (Friends of the Public Garden, 2000).

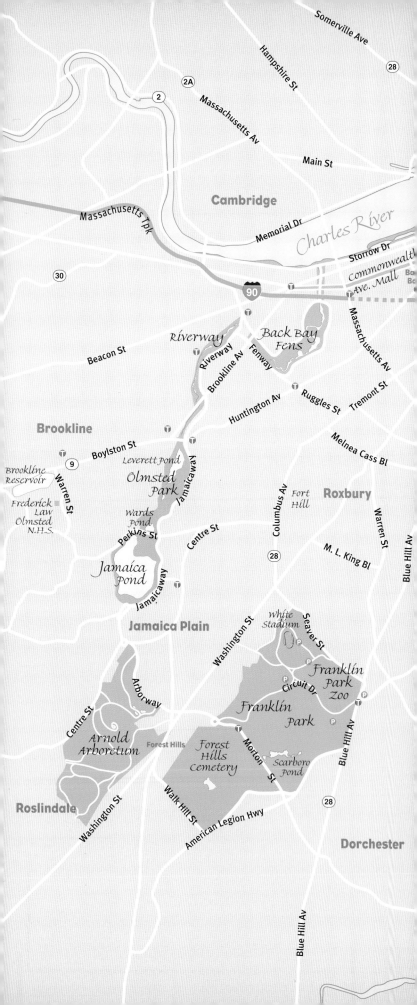

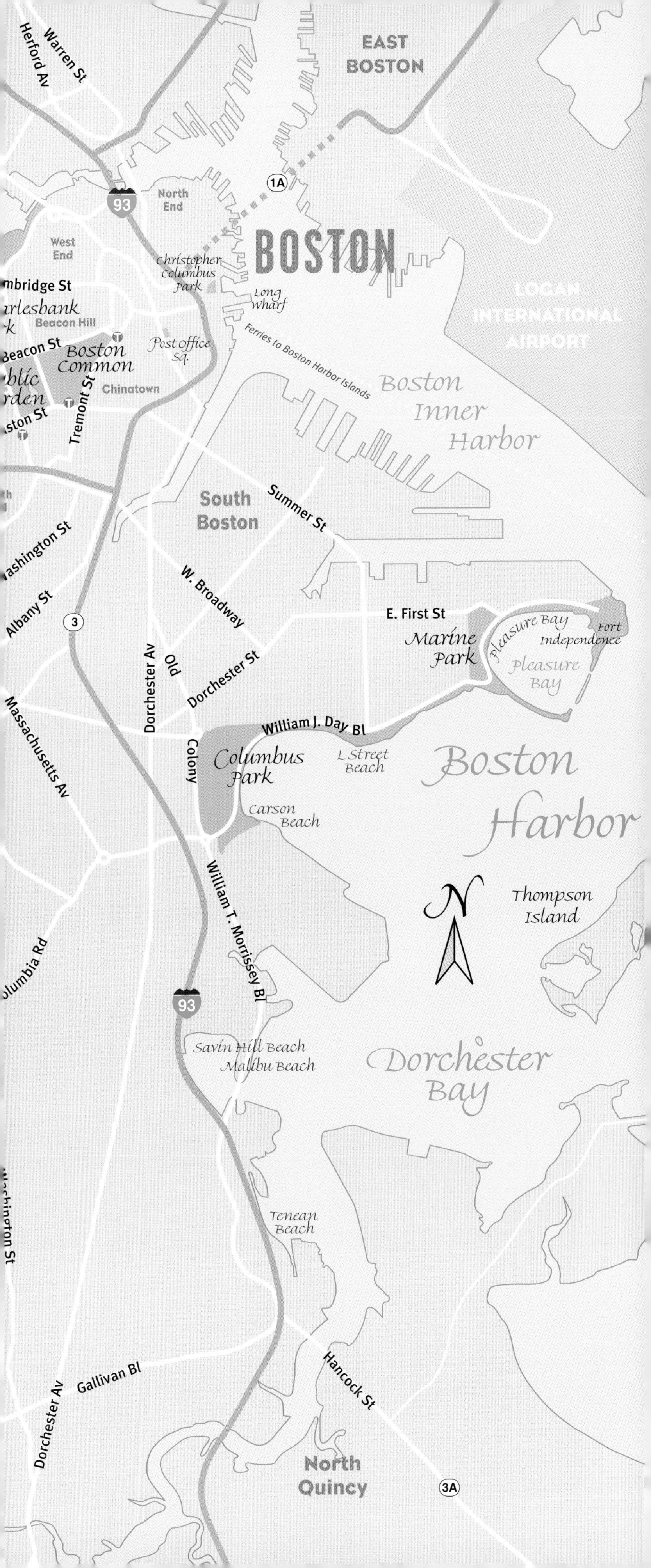

EAST
BOSTON

I-93

North
End

1A

BOSTON

West
End

Christopher
Columbus
Park

Long
Wharf

LOGAN
INTERNATIONAL
AIRPORT

mbridge St

rlesbank
rk

Beacon Hill

Beacon St

Boston
Common

blic
rden

Post Office
Sq.

Chinatown

Ferries to Boston Harbor Islands

Boston
Inner
Harbor

ton St

Tremont St

South
Boston

Summer St

Washington St

W. Broadway

E. First St

Marine
Park

Pleasure Bay

Fort
Independence

Albany St

3

Dorchester Av

Old

Dorchester St

William J. Day Bl

L Street
Beach

Pleasure
Bay

Boston

Massachusetts Av

Colony

Columbus
Park

Carson
Beach

Harbor

N

Thompson
Island

lumbia Rd

William T. Morrissey Bl

I-93

93

Savin Hill Beach
Malibu Beach

Dorchester
Bay

shington St

Tenean
Beach

Dorchester Av

Gallivan Bl

Hancock St

North
Quincy

3A

ENJOYING THE PARKS

For a densely populated city crowded onto a small land area, Boston boasts a rich diversity of parks. Tucked in and around the bustling metropolis are lakes, ponds, zoos, botanical gardens, oceanfront beaches, offshore islands, athletic facilities, band shells, skating rinks, picnic fields, riverbanks, bicycle paths, birding trails, campgrounds, community gardens, historic sites, and countless other kinds of outdoor spaces. Several agencies have jurisdiction over the various parks, including the city, the state, the Metropolitan District Commission (MDC), the federal government, and universities and other private not-for-profit institutions.

Rules and Regulations

City of Boston parks are open from 6 a.m. until 11:30 p.m. MDC parks and reservations are generally open from 8 a.m. until 8 p.m.; areas with lighted athletic fields stay open until 11 p.m. from mid-April until mid-November.

MDC beaches are open, with lifeguards on duty, from late June until early September.

The Boston Harbor Islands National Recreation Area is open from 9 a.m. to sunset from early May to mid-October, although events are also scheduled after mid-October on Georges Island.

Most historic public cemeteries are open from dawn to dusk; some are closed except by appointment. Forest Hills Cemetery is open daily from 7:30 a.m. until dusk. Grave rubbings are not allowed in the historic cemeteries.

The Arnold Arboretum is open daily from dawn to dusk.

Park rules require that visitors do no harm to landscape or wildlife. Picking flowers, cutting branches, removing plants or rocks, disturbing birds' nests or eggs, and injuring or removing any wild animal or bird are prohibited.

Also prohibited: alcohol, firearms, fireworks, sitting on or climbing over any fence or monument, walking on the flower beds, sitting or lying in any nondesignated areas in the Public Garden, and making public speeches or distributing printed matter anywhere in the Public Garden or within 25 feet of playgrounds or athletic fields in any Boston parks, including the Frog Pond on the Boston Common.

Dogs in the Parks

Dogs must be kept on a leash no longer than eight feet. As everywhere in the city, owners are required to clean up after their dogs. No dogs are allowed at all in the Public Garden, with the exception of dogs that assist blind people.

Finding Your Way

Park information is available at the visitor information center on the Tremont Street side of Boston Common, or by calling 617-635-4505. Boston Park Rangers, distinguished by their brown uniforms and Smokey Bear hats, are also stationed in the signature parks. Some patrol on horseback.

Safety

A few Boston parks, particularly the Back Bay Fens and Franklin Park, have suffered from a perception that the surrounding neighborhoods are high-crime areas. This may have once been true, but most of these neighborhoods have improved considerably in the last decade. In recent years, the city has reported virtually no crimes against persons in its parks. There is almost constant foot traffic on the pathways in the Boston Common, Public Garden, Commonwealth Avenue Mall, and around Jamaica Pond. In some parks, most notably the Fens, however, it is not advisable to walk alone at night.

Several law enforcement agencies have jurisdiction over Boston's parks. To report a crime, call 911 to reach the Boston Police. City parks are also patrolled by the Boston Park Rangers, whose direct telephone number is 617-635-7383; and by

the Boston Common, one in the Back Bay Fens, and three in Franklin Park. There is a skateboard park on Reservation Road, a parkway south of Franklin Park. The Frog Pond Pavilion on the Boston Common serves as a wading pool in the summer and a skating rink in the winter. Children predominate there in both seasons.

A wildly popular destination for kids inside Boston's parks is the *Make Way for Ducklings* sculpture in the Public Garden, featuring child-size bronze likenesses of Mr. and Mrs. Mallard from the famous children's book, followed closely by Jack, Kack, Lack, Mack, Nack, Ouack, Pack, and Quack.

The statues are the final stop of a family-friendly walking tour run by the nonprofit Historic Neighborhoods Foundation (617-426-1885), which follows the route of Mr. and Mrs. Mallard and their offspring. The famous Swan Boats nearby are as much a must for children as they are for parents. And the Granary Burying Ground is the final resting place of Elizabeth Vergoose, the woman reputed to be Mother Goose. Paul Revere, John Hancock, and Samuel Adams also are buried there.

The Boston Park Rangers (617-635-7487) run free programs for children, including readings of *Make Way for Ducklings* in the Public Garden, wilderness tours, botany classes, visits with the mounted rangers' horses, tours of the horse stables inside Franklin Park, and fishing trips to Jamaica Pond.

The Back Bay Fens serves as the front yard of the Museum of Fine Arts, which welcomes children with a self-guided activity book that includes Mystery of the Mummy, a sort of scavenger hunt through the ancient Egyptian galleries. The preserved Civil War fort in the Boston Harbor Islands National Recreation Area, complete with dungeons and ghost stories, is also a favorite with young visitors.

In the summer, free concerts are given at the Parkman Bandstand on the Boston Common and at the Hatch Shell on the Esplanade, where family-oriented films are shown on Friday nights at sunset.

the Municipal Police, 617-635-4916. The Boston Harbor Islands National Recreation Area is managed jointly by the National Park Service, the Massachusetts Department of Environmental Management, the MDC, and the United States Coast Guard.

Food and Restrooms

Licensed vendors sell food and drinks along the Charles Street side of the Boston Common in the spring, summer, and fall. The Frog Pond Jazz Café on the Common features a snack bar with outdoor seating and live jazz in the summer. For information, call 617-635-2121. Also in the summer, Emerson College operates an outdoor café along the edge of the Common on the corner of Boylston and Tremont streets. There are snack bars at the Jamaica Pond boathouse (617-522-6258) and at the William J. Devine Golf Course clubhouse inside Franklin Park (617-265-4084).

Public restrooms are few and far between in Boston and its parks. Restrooms are located at the Frog Pond Pavilion and visitor information center on the Boston Common, in the Jamaica Pond boathouse, at the William J. Devine Golf Course clubhouse inside Franklin Park, and in the field house in John Joseph Moakley Park. The Moakley field house is open only in the summer. Restrooms are also planned for Christopher Columbus Park.

Fun for the Kids

There are no fewer than 144 tot lots in Boston's parks, including one on

A History of Boston and Its Parks

Boston's population of barely more than half a million ranks it a distant 21st in the United States. But its influence has historically been vastly disproportionate to its small size.

This historic city is home to some of America's foremost educational, medical, and cultural institutions, has produced some of the nation's intellectual and political giants, and was predominant in the very founding of the world's greatest democracy. It has amassed great wealth in industries ranging from fishing and whaling and the China trade to banking and technology. And it has one of the finest systems of urban parks in the world, including the first public park, first public garden, and first arboretum open to the public.

For all of this, however, Boston's parks had surprisingly ignoble beginnings. The Boston Common, the first public park in America, proved a convenient spot for hanging religious dissenters. The Public Garden, Back Bay Fens, and Riverway were built to mask a foul-smelling sewage problem. And Franklin Park was rooted in Bostonians' longtime (and continuing) jealous rivalry with New York, whose Central Park had been created to extraordinary popular acclaim.

But what was mostly behind the development of parks in Boston was the fact that from the time it was claimed by the Puritans in 1630, the city has been an overcrowded, densely populated, finite spit of land—a problem that remains evident to this day in its famous traffic congestion and high housing prices.

When the city's earliest settlers arrived on the shores of the New World, they found a peninsula of only 783 acres, consisting of the present-day North End and Beacon Hill. Over the years, energetic Bostonians expanded their city significantly by filling in the Charles River embankment and the harbor front. As crowding worsened in the 19th century, alarmed civic leaders set aside open space wherever they could find it (within the confines of Yankee thrift, of course, which discouraged them from spending too much on the land). And while some of this space was nibbled away in the 20th century, it is now virtually sacrosanct, considered one of the most important legacies left by the city's forebears. Today, though Boston continues to be confined to a land area smaller than the island of Martha's Vineyard, it boasts 5,000 acres of public recreation space.

Earliest Days

Crowding and pollution led to the very founding of this town. The Puritans who settled in Charlestown in 1630 quickly overtaxed the single available water well, which soon became fouled. So the Puritans moved across the harbor to what was then called the Shawmut Peninsula, now downtown Boston. There a single resident, the Reverend William Blackstone, had discovered a freshwater spring and built a cabin. The Puritans paid Blackstone 30 pounds for his land, which they set aside as a common area for grazing cattle. This became the Boston Common, still almost exactly the same size and shape as it was nearly 400 years ago. From small homes and farms around the city, cows and sheep were led to the Common to graze, following the jumbled paths that now comprise the city's tangled road system, and Quakers and other religious dissenters were hanged from a giant elm tree there.

Eventually the Common became a place for residents to take the air along formal walkways laid out beginning in 1675. It was also used as a military training field, and as a camp for occupying British as the struggle for independence from the mother country loomed.

Urban Repose

The success of that war began a time of confidence and economic prosperity. The city's population more than tripled between 1790 and 1825, from 18,000 to 58,000, after having been flat for the previous five decades. It more than doubled again by 1850, thanks largely to Irish immigration. Ten years later, there were nearly 180,000 residents. Even though the land area was slowly pushed out into the water, the city was becoming intolerably crowded

Parkland in Boston in 1873 was clearly at a premium, as shown in this detail of a panoramic map published by Currier & Ives. In the near distance, Boston Common and the Public Garden extend eastward from the domed State Capitol building. In the far distance, Mt. Auburn Cemetery sits north of the Charles River in Cambridge.

11

with homes, churches, and public buildings.

The public's earliest relief from growing communal claustrophobia was in eternal repose—or, more precisely, newly voguish garden cemeteries. Cemeteries like Mount Auburn in Cambridge began to be built, with rolling hills, ponds, ledges, trees, and shrubs. The first large-scale designed landscape in the United States open to the public, Mount Auburn was established in 1831. The public flocked to these open spaces; the dead were practically afterthoughts. Here again, the development was primarily pragmatic. In a city squeezed for space, existing urban cemeteries were so congested that graves were being reused, with the remains of the dead laid on top of each other. But there were also philosophical elements. A new idea of the therapeutic value of peaceful natural surroundings was gaining favor. In 1847, a 72-acre plot of land was purchased in the then suburb of Roxbury. There, Forest Hills Cemetery was laid out, with carefully planned landscapes and grand sculptures marking the final resting places of the city's richest and most influential people.

Still, Roxbury was at the time a long way from downtown Boston. And as the population grew and grew, the Boston Common began to be converted into a refuge for people, not cattle. Tree-lined paths, or malls, were built around the periphery, and cows were banned, replaced by fountains, statues, and public art. Six hundred trees were planted, and a decorative cast-iron fence built. The increasingly affluent residents of Beacon Hill would promenade around the Common in the evening.

By then, the American public parks movement was well under way. Prospect Park was being planned in Brooklyn, and Baltimore and Philadelphia had both started work on large parks. But what made the Boston Brahmins' blue blood boil was the development of Central Park, then under construction in New York. "While other cities are expending fabulous amounts in the improvements of parks, squares, gardens, and promenades, what should we do? To be behind in these matters would not only be discreditable to our city, but positively injurious to our commercial prosperity," a citizens' committee wrote.

From Swamps to Parks

Boston responded by creating the Public Garden at the site of what was once a stagnant tidal flat at the far end of the Common. A referendum to set aside the spot was approved by a margin of sixty to one, and the Garden's current-day lagoon, flower beds, and trees were laid out. But at one end of this elegant spot

Visitors stroll through an idyllic setting at Forest Pond in Mount Auburn Cemetery in this c. 1845 engraving by William H. Bartlett.

River and through Brookline, Brighton, and Cambridge, through which people could ride directly into the open country. This was the rudimentary beginning of the Emerald Necklace, a chain of parks and parkways that would ring the city.

After a series of false starts and blunders, the parks commission finally turned for help to the man who had created Central Park itself: Frederick Law Olmsted. Olmsted, who had friends in Cambridge, had been watching the development of Boston's parks with interest. Fed up with the politicking that had accompanied his New York projects, the native New Englander was clearly pining to be consulted for his help. "It is possible I may yet be of service to you," he had hinted in a letter to the parks commission.

Hiring Olmsted was the most important decision the commission ever made.

Olmsted Takes Charge

Known as the father of landscape architecture, Frederick Law Olmsted personally designed many of America's most famous green spaces. Yet Boston's Emerald Necklace, built between 1878 and 1895, was to be his favorite project.

Olmsted was influenced by the English "pleasure parks," with their rolling natural landscapes. But he also was moved by the philosophy of the Massachusetts transcendentalist Ralph Waldo Emerson, who wrote in his essay "Nature" that man's spiritual side was connected to his physical surroundings. Olmsted saw parks as places where people could restore harmony and calmness to their lives. "We want a ground to which people may easily go when their day's work is done, and where they may stroll for an hour, seeing, hearing, and feeling nothing of the bustle and jar of the streets," said Olmsted; "where they shall, in effect, find the city put far away from them."

But Olmsted's more immediate problem was to create a major work of drainage and engineering that would eliminate the smelly swamp beyond the Back Bay. He built a tidal gate to control the water level, and a series of man-made rivers and ponds to hold the overflow from heavy rains. His engineering would be disguised as a park, which Olmsted

remained a fetid swamp, unworthy of the city's emergent influence and wealth. So plans were made for this "back bay" to be filled in and a whole new neighborhood created. Its centerpiece would be a grand Parisian-style boulevard called Commonwealth Avenue, with a 100-foot-wide mall down the middle. It immediately became Boston's most prestigious address, and the wealthiest residents competed to see who could build the grandest homes there.

But as the city pushed outward, the sewage problem grew worse. Nor did the acres of new landfill do much to ease the overcrowding, dominated as it was by large mansions for the elite. That problem, too, was about to be solved. Once the powerful new residents of the Back Bay got a whiff of the polluted, flood-prone tidal salt marsh just to the west, there were calls to fill it in. The influential class was also conscious of the critical scarcity of open space. Despite the development of the Public Garden and Commonwealth Avenue Mall, Boston still had only 115 acres of open space, compared with more than 1,300 acres in New York and Brooklyn.

In 1875, a parks commission was appointed to convert the reeking tidal basin to a park. At the same time, a lawyer named Uriel Crocker proposed a long, continuous stretch of green space along the Charles

Frederick Law Olmsted

Designer of Boston's Park System

In his long life, Frederick Law Olmsted would come to be considered the father of American landscape architecture. He would personally design Central and Prospect parks in New York City, the grounds of the U.S. Capitol Building, and 500 other projects. The firm he founded with his sons would eventually work on nearly 5,000 assignments in 45 states and several countries. Yet Boston's Emerald Necklace was to be his favorite achievement—and his last. "Nothing else compares in importance to us with the Boston work," he wrote in 1893, two years before he retired, when construction on the Boston parks was finally also nearing its end.

A native New Englander, Olmsted was born in 1822 and raised in Hartford, Connecticut. The son of a dry goods merchant, he was trained as a civil engineer but worked at many jobs before he found his true vocation. He clerked in a dry goods store in New York and served as a sailor on a bark to China. He worked as a journalist, and was a cofounder of *The Nation*. Finally, as he apprenticed at several farms, he began to find his calling. He attended courses at Yale in chemistry and scientific farming and began to plan for an entirely new career, which he called landscape architecture. He was 35 years old.

Olmsted saw parks as places of rest where people could restore the balance of harmony and calm in their lives, reconnect with their communities, and escape increasingly congested cities. He called them pleasure grounds. "We want a ground . . . where [people] shall, in effect, find the city put far away from them."

◆ ◆ ◆

Using the influence he had gained as a journalist, Olmsted got himself appointed superintendent of New York's Central Park in 1857, just as designs for the 843-acre park in the middle of Manhattan were being solicited by city leaders. English-born architect Calvert Vaux invited him to collaborate on a design, and the team prepared a layout called Greensward, which was ultimately selected as the winning plan.

With that triumph, Olmsted was sought after to design other projects, including Mount Royal Park in Montreal and Belle Isle Park in Detroit. He laid out the campuses of Amherst College, Stanford University, and the University of California at Berkeley, and designed the first planned suburb, in Riverside, Illinois. He was a leader in the campaign to protect Niagara Falls, and worked to preserve what is now Yosemite National Park. During the Civil War, he headed the U.S. Sanitary Commission, predecessor to the American Red Cross.

But politics was dampening his enthusiasm for work in New York City. Dejected by infighting over the park projects there, he came to Cambridge to spend two consecutive summers with friends, and took an interest in the ongoing spirited discussions over a new system of parks for Boston.

Always (and still) a rival of New York, Boston wanted a preserve as grand as Central Park. Densely populated, confined to a peninsula, the city had little space, however. Olmsted, who served as an informal advisor, was closely involved in a final report that recommended several green spaces of varying sizes and types, connected by parkways, running from the existing Boston Common to a new park in Jamaica Plain. But he was not invited to design them. Instead, the parks commission held a competition like New York's, and invited Olmsted to serve as a judge. He declined, adding prophetically, "It is possible I may yet be of service to you" in a professional capacity.

Sure enough, the winning design was amateurish, and Olmsted was asked in 1878 to step in under a long-term consulting contract. His first project was the Back Bay Fens, where the immediate problem was not necessarily creating a park, but eliminating a sewage problem that had created a festering cesspool. Olmsted designed a series of underground conduits and gates to remove the sewage, and created an artificial salt marsh and a winding stream with boat landings and walking bridges. In practice, it was not among his many successes. The system worked poorly, and when a dam was later built on the Charles River, the water turned from salt to fresh, killing Olmsted's marsh. The Fens has since been significantly altered from the original design.

In 1883, Olmsted moved permanently from New York to the Boston suburb of Brookline, where many of his friends already lived, including Charles Sprague Sargent, who would become director of the Arnold Arboretum, and architect and frequent Olmsted collaborator H. H. Richardson. His estate, which he called Fairsted, also housed his office, one of the earliest professional practices of landscape architecture in the world. Among his students and successors were his sons, John Charles and Frederick Law Olmsted, Jr. The firm operated out of the same office until 1980, when the site was acquired by the National Park Service.

By the time it was completed, Boston's "Emerald Necklace" of parks would total more than 2,000 acres, including seven major green spaces (the Boston Common, the Public Garden, Back Bay Fens, Muddy River, Jamaica Park, Arnold Arboretum, and Franklin Park), connecting parkways (the Fenway, the Riverway, the Jamaicaway, and the Arborway), and the Commonwealth Avenue Mall. The arboretum was incorporated into the design thanks almost exclusively to lobbying by Olmsted, who had agreed to lay it out free at the behest of his equally stubborn neighbor, Sargent. Harvard, which owned the property, and the city, which was being asked to pay for the improvements, finally if reluctantly agreed.

(The Common, the Public Garden, and Commonwealth Avenue Mall predated Olmsted, but were also made a part of his plan.)

After nearly 20 years of work, the system was finally finished with the opening of Franklin Park in 1895, the same year Olmsted would retire because of failing health. (His other final major project was the World's Columbian Exposition in Chicago in 1893.) Senile, he was eventually confined to McLean Asylum in Belmont. He would die there on August 28, 1903. But his influence was acclaimed in his own time—and had to be evident to him, even as he breathed his last.

For he had designed the asylum's grounds.

Frederick Law Olmsted

called the Back Bay Fens, after the marshlands or "fens" of eastern England.

It was an enormous challenge that took more than a decade to complete. Equally frustrating was the slow progress of adding other parks. In the 1870s, the nation was in a deep economic recession, made worse in Boston by the great fire of 1872, which had wiped out the financial district. Olmsted conspired with Charles Sprague Sargent, director of Harvard's Arnold Arboretum, to make the 394-acre Jamaica Plain collection of plants and trees a link in the Emerald Necklace. In exchange, they proposed, the city would pay to prepare the grounds, build roads and footpaths, and provide police patrols.

Despite resistance from both Harvard and the city council, Olmsted and the well-connected Sargent got their plan approved, with considerable help from the emergent class of wealthy gentlemen farmers who raised gardens on their large estates. The city bought the land and leased it back for a dollar a year for 1,000 years to Harvard, which agreed to keep it open to the public. It became the first public arboretum in the United States.

In 1883, Olmsted moved permanently from New York to the Boston suburb of Brookline. By then the Emerald Necklace was well under way. The Back Bay Fens finally opened, to be followed by the Riverway, a combination park and parkway bisected by the Muddy River that divides Boston from Brookline. Part of what Olmsted called the Muddy River Improvement is now named for him: Olmsted Park. Next was added Jamaica Pond, a deep glacial kettle hole and its surrounding grounds, which connect Olmsted Park with the Arnold Arboretum. The end of the chain is Franklin Park, Olmsted's 527-acre pride and joy—his best work, according to his stepson, John C. Olmsted. This was to be a landmark "country park," a quiet, passive space where urban residents would be reminded of the gentle pleasures of rural life.

The Emerald Necklace, 2,000 acres of green space, gardens, ponds, and parks, is now listed on the National Register of Historic Places. But not all of this extraordinary system has worked out as planned. The drainage system in the Back Bay Fens later had to be replaced. The connecting link between the Fens and Commonwealth Avenue was effectively broken by the construction of an overpass, and between the Fens and the

This c. 1894 photograph shows a horse-drawn roller leveling the roadbed for what would become the Circuit Drive in Franklin Park. A total of 6 miles of roadway was constructed in this painstaking manner.

Riverway, by a parking lot (since removed, with the link restored). Because of economic limitations, parts of Franklin Park were never developed according to plan. Pressure from various interest groups resulted in the conversion of part of the park into a golf course and part of it into a zoo.

Still, so popular were these parks that in 1893 they helped spawn the creation of the Metropolitan District Commission, the first regional organization of public open space in the United States, pushed by Olmsted disciple Charles Eliot, who was also the son of a president of Harvard. The MDC runs the Esplanade along the Charles River, Boston Harbor beaches, and other metropolitan-area parks, wilderness reservations, and recreational facilities.

The Parks Today

Today the Boston Parks and Recreation Department oversees 2,200 acres of park land including 215 parks and playgrounds, 65 squares, urban woodlands, and street trees, as well as three active cemeteries, 16 historic burying grounds, and two golf courses. The MDC controls 20,000 acres of woodlands, wetlands, and urban parklands; 120,000 acres of watershed area; and 162 miles of parkways joining the parks and reservations much as Olmsted's parkways connect the links along the Emerald Necklace. The MDC park at Castle Island in South Boston is one of Olmsted's few coastal works, at the historic site of the nation's oldest military fortification.

Mid-20th century neglect did great damage to these parks; but since the 1990s pathways have been improved, new trees planted, signage updated, bridges repaired, and boardwalks and buildings renovated. In late 1997, the Emerald Necklace Conservancy was established. Ironically, it was based on the models of the Prospect Park Alliance in Brooklyn and the Central Park Conservancy in New York. Already tens on millions of dollars have been spent restoring Boston's parks to their 19th-century splendor for a new generation of 21st-century devotees.

Emerald Necklace Conservatory
617-722-9823
www.emeraldnecklace.org

THE
EMERALD
NECKLACE

Boston Common

The nation's oldest public park, the Boston Common, was created four years after the Puritans arrived, an outgrowth of the English village institution of a common land for grazing cattle. Now the anchor of the Emerald Necklace, it is one of the most historic places in America.

The Common was the site of drills by the first military company in the Western Hemisphere, the first Mass said in North America by Pope John Paul II, even the first American football game. It has also been the site of gatherings for and against everything from abolition to abortion,

A vital green space in the middle of the city's most compactly settled neighborhood, the Common boasts two other things in short supply in Boston: a parking garage, buried beneath it; and public rest rooms, in the visitor center on the Tremont Street side and at the Frog Pond Pavilion. There is also a subway hidden underneath the park–America's first, of course.

Colonial Days

The first white resident of what was then known only as the Shawmut Peninsula was William Blackstone, who was perfectly content to live a solitary life there with his library of 200 books in a cabin he built in 1625, near what is now the Common's Charles Street Gate. The Puritans, meanwhile, settled a comfortable distance away in Charlestown, where they soon encountered a significant problem: There was no evident source of drinkable water. The reclusive Blackstone reluctantly invited the hapless little band of fellow Englishmen to his side of the harbor, where he had a pure freshwater well. Then he almost immediately moved away, "to be as free of the Governance of the Puritans as that of the King," becoming the first in Boston's long and continuing line of curmudgeons.

The Puritans bought 50 acres from Blackstone for 30 pounds "for a trayning field . . . & for the feeding of Cattell." This became the Common, which is still almost the same size and shape as it was then. A mere two acres or so have been whittled away over the nearly four centuries by the widening of adjacent streets, and other minor changes.

Each Puritan householder was assessed six shillings to pay for the land, originally called the Commonage, and an ordinance was put into law allowing up to 70 milk cows or 270 sheep to be grazed there at any one time; there was a shepherd, and a public herdsman who was paid 2 shillings per cow. Later the Common was protected permanently from being sold or subdivided without the consent of a majority of voters.

Another law banned the cutting of trees, though most had already been removed by the Native Americans. As a result, the Common was a largely treeless, gently rolling, irregularly shaped scrubland flaring out in the direction of what is now Charles Street, then an unappealing marshland where the Charles River rose at high tide. At low tide, boys—including a young Benjamin Franklin—fished, clammed, and angled in the mudflats. There were originally four hills and three ponds, of which only Frog Pond and Flagstaff Hill remain. Most of the population of the town lived near the markets of the modern-day North End. The Common was, for all intents and purposes, the city's unremarkable back yard.

Blackstone's point about "governance," was proved for him when the Puritans set to work almost immediately hanging pirates, thieves, witches, and Quakers on the Common, including Mary Dyer, a Quaker who believed that it was possible to pray to God without the intervention of a minister. A statue of Dyer, who was executed in 1660, now stands in front of the Massachusetts State House.

Most of the hangings took place from a limb of a huge tree called the Great Elm until it was replaced in 1769

Mary Dyer being led to execution on the Common.

The *TOWN of BOSTON IN New England by Capt John Bonner 1722*

The Bonner map of 1722 shows the Common located outside the city proper to keep the town's gunpowder (stored in the Powder House) at a safe distance.

by a gallows, where the public punishments continued until the gallows was moved quietly to South Boston in 1812. Damaged by a storm in 1869, the Great Elm finally blew down in 1876.

The Common began its transition from pasture to park as early as 1675, when its first formal walkway was laid out. It also became a popular gathering place. Troops departed from there for the French and Indian War, there was a huge bonfire to celebrate the repeal of the Stamp act in 1766, effigies were burned in protest of the tax on tea, and the colonial militia mustered for the Revolution.

In 1768, nearly 2,000 British soldiers began an eight-year encampment on the Common, digging trenches and putting up a sturdy granite storage building for their ordnance on what became known as Powder House Hill (now Flagstaff Hill). On April 18, 1775, the redcoats marched down to the mudflats and boarded longboats for the trip to Cambridge and their fateful march to Lexington and Concord,

a historic moment commemorated by a plaque on the gate between the Common and the Public Garden. In 1776, the British lifted their siege of Boston under the threat of American cannon. Bonfires were lit again on the Common to celebrate the surrender at Yorktown.

After encamping on Boston Common for eight years, British troops evacuate the city in 1776 under the threat of American cannons on Dorchester Heights.

A Park at Last

As Boston grew more crowded, Bostonians exhibited a newfound enthusiasm for their public spaces—or, more accurately, their only public space—the Boston Common. By the early 19th century, tree-lined paths, or malls, were built around the periphery of the Common, beginning with the Tremont Street Mall, where couples would promenade together in the evenings and on weekends. The mall was renamed in honor of the French Marquis de Lafayette in 1825, when Lafayette and other Revolutionary War veterans marched from the Common to Charlestown exactly 50 years after the British had taken the same route at the outset of the Battle of Bunker Hill. A monument to Lafayette and the parade was built nearby 100 years after that.

By 1830, cows were banned from Boston Common, replaced by fountains, statues, and public art. Six hundred trees were planted, and a decorative cast-iron fence built (only the section of the fence along Beacon Street remains). There were also more and bigger public spectacles, though few as noteworthy as the one to celebrate the completion of the Boston public water system.

Of Water and Slaves

The supply of fresh water had continued to be a problem long after Blackstone sold the Puritans his well. Deeper wells, rain barrels, and a spring on Boston Common continued to be used until the late 18th century, when a system of wooden pipes carved out of tree trunks was built to carry water to the city from Jamaica Pond. But the little pond, which grew increasingly polluted, couldn't keep up with the demands of a population which was by then approaching 50,000.

To meet the demands of the growing city, a tributary of the Sudbury River in Natick was dammed up to form a reservoir called Lake Cochituate, and an aqueduct was built to carry water to the metropolis. With dramatic flair, the first water drawn from Lake Cochituate spewed 90 feet into the air from a fountain in Frog Pond on Boston Common on October 25, 1848, accompanied by choirs, church bells, and artillery fire, before an appreciative throng of 100,000.

More serious events were also being held by then—namely anti-slavery protests. They would give way to recruiting speeches as the Civil War came. Departing volunteers paraded on the Common, including the 54th Massachusetts Regiment, the first black regiment recruited in the North. The 54th, whose exploits were the subject of the movie *Glory*, is commemorated by the single greatest monument on Boston Common, the Robert Gould Shaw and 54th Regiment Memorial by sculptor Augustus Saint-Gaudens.

By 1895, with the population continuing to increase, the traffic on Boston's streets was so bad that the city built a subway for the trolleys underneath the Common. It was an engineering marvel, but it had significant effects on the park above. Graves in the Central Burying Ground had to be dug up and moved, and the iron fencing along Tremont Street was taken down, never to be replaced.

The subway's second station, at Boylston Street, took away another corner of the park. As automobile traffic increased, Tremont, Boylston, Park, and Charles Streets all were widened, chipping away still more at the Common. Centuries of wear and tear had also taken their toll.

The view to the northeast over the Public Garden and Boston Common reveals a refreshing abundance of trees and greenery.

Olmsted and Company

In 1910, Frederick Law Olmsted's landscape architecture firm, now under the direction of Olmsted's son and namesake Frederick Law Olmsted, Jr., took on the three-year job of renovating the Common. The soil was replenished and trees replanted in some sections, though it was impossible to plant above the subway because the soil there was only two feet deep. Later, when a three-level underground parking garage was added, the Common would have structures buried under 17 percent of its total area. Soil depths above the garage are also shallow, at only about four feet.

Today there are 743 trees on Boston Common, about 40 percent fewer than in the mid-1850s and 10 percent fewer than in 1910. (Dutch elm disease and the aging process have killed some of the trees.) Still, many of the trees are hung with colored lights at Christmas, making one of the prettier downtown sights.

Trees might have been impossible to plant, but victory gardens sprouted everywhere on the Common during World War I. In World War II, much of the remaining iron fencing went for scrap metal. But the fences had by then become superfluous. Rallies attracted larger and larger crowds. Charles Lindbergh spoke to 200,000 after his solo flight to Paris, and there were anti–Vietnam War protests and civil rights rallies including one led by Martin Luther King, Jr., in 1965. And in 1979, when Pope John Paul II celebrated his first Mass in North America, 400,000 people came to the Common to hear it, ignoring a driving downpour. To this day, permits are issued for 200 events per year on Boston Common.

A Walking Tour of Boston Common

Most visitors think Boston Common must be square. It isn't. Like the rest of Boston's downtown, it was laid out centuries ago according to the contours of the land and the direction of the cow paths. Logic and geometry have little to do with it. The park begins at its narrowest point along Park Street between Tremont and Beacon streets and flares out toward Charles Street in the direction of the Public Garden. It is bounded on a fifth side by Boylston Street.

Closed in as it is by this historic city, Boston Common is as interesting for what's around it as for what's in it. Just across Beacon Street, for instance, is the Massachusetts State House, built in 1798, which Oliver Wendell Holmes said in 1858 was

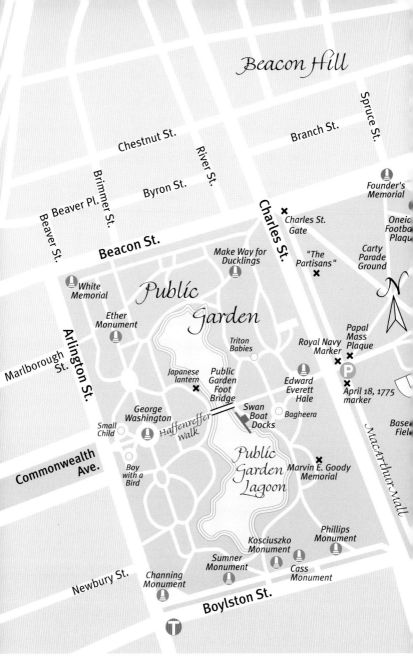

Chestnut St.

Branch St.

Spruce St.

River St.

Brimmer St.

Byron St.

Beaver Pl.

Beaver St.

Charles St.

Founder's Memorial

× Charles St. Gate

Oneic Footba Plaqu

Beacon St.

Make Way for Ducklings

"The Partisans" ×

Carty Parade Ground

White Memorial

Public Garden

Ether Monument

Triton Babies

Royal Navy Marker ×

Papal Mass Plaque ×

N

Marlborough St.

Arlington St.

Japanese lantern ×

Public Garden Foot Bridge

Edward Everett Hale

P

April 18, 1775 marker

George Washington

Swan Boat Docks

Bagheera ●

MacArthur Mall

Base Fiel

Small Child

Haffenreffer walk

Commonwealth Ave.

Boy with a Bird

Public Garden Lagoon

Marvin E. Goody Memorial

Phillips Monument

Kosciuszko Monument

Newbury St.

Channing Monument

Sumner Monument

Cass Monument

Boylston St.

T

the "hub of the solar system." A block from Boston Common near the corner of Summer and Washington streets is a bronze medallion in the sidewalk that purports to mark the exact center of the universe. Whichever is the correct spot, the Boston Common is right smack in the middle. And its other neighbors, in addition to the gold-domed State House designed by Charles Bulfinch—the architect who also designed the U.S. Capitol—include the Park Street Church, the Arlington Street Church, the headquarters of the Unitarian Universalist Association, and the first blocks of Beacon Street, with some of the finest Federal-style architecture in America.

America's First Subway

Start your visit at the Park Street station of the MBTA, the nation's oldest subway station. By the late 19th century, Boston's narrow, crooked streets were so clogged it was said pedestrians could walk to work on the roofs of the gridlocked trolley cars. This notorious traffic is what prompted the city to build the first subway system in the Western Hemisphere, which opened in 1897.

Opposite the station is the Blackstone Memorial Tablet, erected in 1913 to commemorate the founding of the Boston Common in 1634. The inscription relies on the testimony of town elders remembering 50 years later that "in or about the year of our Lord one thousand six hundred thirty four, the then present inhabitants of said town of Boston of

America's first subway was opened under the Boston Public Garden in 1897 to keep electric trolley cars free from gridlock. This c. 1904 photo shows two trolleys descending beneath the park.

whom the Honorable John Winthrop Esquire, governor of the Colony, was chiefe, did treate and agree with Mr. William Blackstone for the purchase of his Estate and rights to any Lands lying within said neck of Land called Boston after which purchase the Town laid out a plan for a trayning field which ever since and now is used for that purpose and for the feeding of cattell."

Just behind the station entrances is the monument to the Marquis de Lafayette, by John F. Paramino, which marks the 100th anniversary of Lafayette's march with other vet-

An ocean god and a sea goddess lend an appropriately aquatic theme to the Renaissance-style Brewer Fountain.

erans to Bunker Hill in 1825. That, in turn, celebrated the 50th anniversary of the Battle of Bunker Hill. This plaza and the adjacent walkway, originally called the Tremont Street Mall, is now known as Lafayette Mall.

Brewer Fountain and Barry Monument

Next is the prominent Renaissance-style Brewer Fountain, designed by Paul Liénard with statues by Matthew Moreau. The figures represent Poseidon, god of the oceans; his wife, Amphitrite, goddess of the sea; and the thwarted lovers Acis and Galatea. The fountain is named for Boston merchant Gardner Brewer, who brought it home from the Paris Exposition of 1867 and gave it to the city the next year.

The next landmark along the Common's Tremont Street side is a monument to Commodore John Barry, known as the father of the American Navy, also the work of Paramino

The 6-foot-4-inch Barry, an Irish Catholic who began his seagoing career as a cabin boy, was commissioned by the Continental Congress to captain the brig *Lexington* in 1775. He was the first to capture a British warship on the high seas, one of more than 20 enemy vessels he would seize before the war was over. He also fought on land at the battles of Trenton and Princeton, and in the last naval battle of the Revolution, aboard the frigate *Alliance* in 1783.

After the war, Barry was appointed by President George Washington to plan and command the U.S. Navy. He lived not in Boston but in Philadelphia, which was more accepting of Roman Catholics at the time. The fact that he was memorialized in Boston more than 150 years after the events that made him famous is due to the fact that by then, Roman Catholics of Irish descent like him were not only present in the city, but prominent. One was the mayor, James Michael Curley.

Visitor Information Center

Just beyond the Barry Monument is the Boston Common Visitor Information Center, which is open from 8:30 a.m. to 5 p.m. (9 a.m. to 5 p.m. on Sundays) every day but Christmas. It also has public rest rooms, which are particularly scarce in this section of the city.

The plaza in front of the visitor center is named for George F. Parkman, who left a bequest of $5 million for the care of the Common and other parks when he died in 1905. Designed by the landscape architect Arthur Shurcliff, the plaza is ringed by the flags of the New England states and by three art deco statues representing Industry, Religion, and Learning. Placed around a central flower bed, they are by brother-in-law sculptors Arcangelo Cascieri (Religion) and Adio DiBiccari (Learning and Industry). DiBiccari's sculptures were exhibited at the highly stylized 1939 New York World's Fair.

Memorials to the American Revolution

Next up is another comparatively plain Paramino: a shallow bas-relief on a huge tablet crowned by an eagle. On the relief is written the entire Declaration of Independence below a representation of its signing at Philadelphia, based on the famous mural by John Trumbull that is in the U.S. Capitol rotunda. Beside that is the Boston Massacre Memorial, a tall pointed column installed in 1888. On the front of the monument is a bronze bas-relief by Robert Kraus depicting the Boston Massacre, in which five Bostonians were killed by panicky British sentries on March 5, 1770. This dispute actually began over the singularly unpatriotic issue of an unpaid bill owed by a soldier to a wigmaker, but

Old headstones in the Central Burying Ground now hide the identities of many underground inhabitants, as the markings have long since worn away.

it was seized upon by activists to drum up opposition to the crown. "From that moment," Daniel Webster later said, "we may date the severance of the British Empire." The hands of one of the victims extends in high relief from the tablet, rubbed to a shine by people shaking it.

At the bottom of the frame is the fallen Crispus Attucks, a free black who was the first to fall; his boot also protrudes. There are also figures symbolizing Revolution breaking the chains of tyranny.

At the corner of Boylston and Tremont streets—once the city's red-light district but now one of its trendiest neighborhoods—is the 40-foot-wide corner of the Common carved away for the MBTA's Boylston Street station, the city's second subway station. On an abandoned siding inside (you'll have to pay the fare) are two of the vintage workhorse streetcars that carried generations of commuters: No. 5734, a boxy 1924 model; and the cigar-shaped No. 3295, designed in 1936. Both have been restored to the color and condition of their daily service through the tunnels and along the network of surface tracks that radiated from the city center.

Central Burying Ground

Round the corner to the Central Burying Ground. Opened in 1754 to help ease crowding at the Granary and King's Chapel cemeteries, the Central was added to the Common in 1839. Foreign visitors and bivouacked British soldiers who died of nothing more heroic than disease are buried beneath these thin slate headstones, whose markings have long since worn away.

So fragile is this cemetery

that it's off-limits, surrounded by an iron fence. But it also is the final resting place of the painter Gilbert Stuart, famous for his many portraits of George Washington—especially the one that appears on dollar bills; and one of America's first composers, William Billings. While the exact locations of their graves are not known, a tablet in memory of Stuart was placed by fellow artists in 1897. The long, grass-covered crypt houses the remains that were removed when Boylston Street was extended to connect with Tremont, lopping off a row of tombs. And the

Kraus's bas-relief on the base of the Boston Massacre Memorial is derived from an image that Paul Revere engraved and distributed shortly after the actual event occurred.

The c. 1912 Parkman bandstand was recently renovated and is still used for musical performances and rallies. The Soldiers and Sailors Monument is seen in the distance.

large grave in the northwest corner contains remains that were unearthed during the construction of the subway in 1895.

Parkman Bandstand and the Flagstaff

Double back to the Parkman Bandstand, also named for George, a neoclassical pavilion with terrazzo floor and pink marble columns, cornice, and dome. Built in 1912 by the firm of Derby, Robinson & Shepard, the bandstand was renovated in 1998 and is used for musical performances and rallies. There was once a pond at this site, alternately known as Cow Pond or Horse Pond. In 1838 it was filled in after cows were no longer allowed to graze here.

Between the bandstand and the baseball diamonds, which border Charles Street, is the Flagstaff. The flagpole was moved here from the Common's Flagstaff Hill in 1866 to make room for the mammoth Soldiers and Sailors Memorial. The flagpole itself dates from 1837. This site once was called the Smoker's Circle, since it was the only place on Boston Common where smoking was allowed.

Round the second baseball diamond and aim for the exit to the Public Garden. There, beside the entrance to the parking garage, is a simple stone commemorating the 1979 visit of Pope John Paul II, when 400,000 people crowded onto Boston Common to hear his first papal Mass in North America. The exit to Charles Street is flanked by two paradoxical historical plaques. One marks the site where British redcoats slipped their boats into the river on their way to Lexington and Concord on April 18, 1775, at the outset of the American Revolution; the other is from the Royal Navy, thanking the residents of Boston for their hospitality during World War II shore leaves. Farther along Charles Street toward Beacon is a contemporary cast metal sculpture called *The Partisans*, by the Polish sculptor Andrzej Pitynski, a Cold War–era tribute to revolutionaries and freedom fighters. Originally put here on temporary loan, it has remained permanently.

Carty Parade Ground

The Charles Street Gate on the corner of Charles and Beacon streets, built in 1836, is the last of five original entrance gates. Just inside this corner is the Carty Parade Ground, laid out in 1852 on the field where the original colonial militia drilled. It was named in 1963 for Thomas Carty, captain of the Ancient and Honorable Artillery Company, the oldest military company in the Western Hemisphere and third-oldest chartered military organization in the world.

The Ancient and Honorable mustered as a voluntary militia on this spot on the first Monday in June of 1638, an event repeated here every year on that date. The company is also sanctioned by the State Department to participate in military events overseas, and it marches in Boston on Patriots Day and Independence Day. James Monroe, Calvin Coolidge, and John F. Kennedy were members; the Ancient and Honorable marched at both JFK's inauguration and his funeral. There are about 860 members now, more than a third of them by right of ancestry.

Founders Memorial

Follow Beacon Street uphill. On the left is the Founders Memorial, another bas-relief by Paramino, in a stone frame by the architect Charles A. Coolidge. It was installed in 1930 to mark the 300th anniversary of the city of Boston. This is the spot where William Blackstone built his house in 1625. It shows Blackstone welcoming John Winthrop's party of Puritans to the Shawmut Peninsula, at which meeting Winthrop purportedly said: "Wee shall be as a City upon a Hill." Blackstone, as we've seen, immediately moved away.

Between the Founders Memorial and Flagstaff Hill is another historic site: the field where the Oneida Football Club of Boston, the first organized football club in the United States, played the first game of football in America in 1862. It is likely the Oneidas actually played a hybrid of soccer and rugby that later became American football. No matter; according to the tablet placed here in 1925 by the 7 surviving members of the 16-member team, "The Oneida goal was never crossed."

Flagstaff Hill

The lone remaining hill inside this park, just ahead, was once called Powder House Hill; on its top, the occupying British built a granite storehouse for their ordnance in 1774. Now called Flagstaff Hill, it is

The Soldiers and Sailors Monument peeks through the fall foliage on Flagstaff Hill. The largest memorial on Boston Common, it commemorates the city's Civil War dead.

Frog Pond Pavilion offers a pleasing oasis for visitors seeking a cooling dip in the summer or ice skating in the winter. A snack bar with outdoor seating overlooks the pond.

the site of the largest monument on Boston Common: the Soldiers and Sailors Memorial by the sculptor Martin Milmore.

Milmore died young, at 39, but not before creating this, the popular Roxbury Soldiers' Monument in Forest Hills Cemetery, and a sphinx at Mount Auburn Cemetery memorializing the Civil War dead. Milmore was himself later memorialized at Forest Hills by Lincoln Memorial sculptor Daniel Chester French.

Dedicated in 1877 before 25,000 doubtless confused Civil War veterans, this massive work looks as if it was designed by a committee of the legislature, which commissioned it. It consists of a 70-foot granite column, flanked by four maidens, at the top of which stands Liberty; four statues near the base, one each representing the Soldier, the Sailor, Peace, and the Muse of History; and four bas-relief plaques depicting the departure of forces for the war, the Battle of Fort Sumter, the return from the war, and for some reason, the Boston Sanitary Commission.

Henry Wadsworth Longfellow and the then governor of Massachusetts, are also memorialized in cameos. Just to muddy the issue further, the monument is flanked by a World War I mine, added in 1921, and a stone in memory of military nurses, placed in 1959.

Frog Pond

Below the hill, beneath the massive horse chestnut trees that drop their shiny fruit in the fall, is something much more straightforward: Frog Pond, the only remaining of the Common's original three ponds. Renovated in 1997 for $4 million into a popular wintertime ice skating rink, the pond converts in the summer to a fountain and in the fall to a reflecting pool. The outdoor rink, which can operate in temperatures of up to 55 degrees, has a surface area of 16,000 square feet. There's also a pavilion with a snack bar, rest rooms, and skate rentals. In warmer months, food is served outside, café-style, and there is sometimes live jazz in the evenings.

This was the site of the celebration on October 25, 1848, inaugurating Boston's public water system. One hundred thousand people watched as a 90-foot fountain was switched on, spewing water that flowed to Boston from Lake Cochituate in Natick through a newly built aqueduct. The fresh supply of water lessened the threat of epidemics and increased the pressure available for fighting fires in the close-built city. (The Cochituate was discontinued as a water source in 1951). The fountain, too, has been restored, and can spray to a height of 70 feet.

Site of the Great Elm

At the far end of the Frog Pond and across Oliver Wendell Holmes path (near where it crosses Mayor's Walk, which runs from Brewer Fountain towards Charles Street) is the site of the Great Elm. Here the Puritans hanged witches, pirates, and religious dissenters. When the elm was damaged in a storm in 1869, and felled by another seven years later, the city mourned. Most by then had forgotten about the public executions from the tree, which had ended in 1769 when a gallows was erected. The gallows was eventually moved to more remote South Boston in 1812.

Guild Steps

Follow Oliver Wendell Holmes Path back toward Beacon Street to see one of the most ornate entrances to the Boston Common: the Guild Steps, built in 1917 to honor three-time governor Curtis Guild, who also served as U.S. ambassador to Russia. The ornate cast-iron railing was restored in 1979. On one of the stone pillars that flank the gate on the Beacon Street side is a bust of Guild himself; on the other, the seal of the Commonwealth of Massachusetts.

54th Regiment Memorial

At the corner of Park and Beacon streets, across from the golden dome of the State House, is the real treasure of the Common: the Robert Gould Shaw and 54th Massachusetts Regiment Memorial by Augustus Saint-Gaudens, one of America's foremost sculptors. The imposing bas-relief bronze commemorates the all-black Civil War company from Boston that became the subject of the movie *Glory*. The bronze relief is dominated by the likeness of the regiment's white colonel, Robert Gould Shaw, who led the July 18, 1863, assault on Fort Wagner in Confederate Charleston, South Carolina. Shaw was killed in the battle, along with 32 of his men. Look closely; when it was built, the monument bore only the names of the regiment's white officers. The names of blacks who died were added when the monument was rededicated in 1982.

The steps leading down from the Shaw monument are dedicated to World War I sailors and soldiers, and the two elm trees to their immediate left are believed to be about 200 years old—one of them planted in 1780 by John Hancock, who lived at the site of what is now the State House.

Boston Common is open from 6 a.m. until 11:30 p.m., though foot traffic continues at all hours.

How to Get to the Common

By subway: Take the MBTA Green or Red lines to Park Street or the Green Line to Boylston Street, or the Red or Orange lines to Downtown Crossing.

By car: From Cambridge, take Memorial Drive to the Longfellow Bridge over the Charles River. At the end of the bridge, take a right onto Charles Street, which runs directly to the Common.

From the west, take the Massa-

In this bronze relief, white Union army colonel Robert Gould Shaw unknowingly leads his all-black regiment to their defeat and his death during the assault on Fort Wagner during the American Civil War. Their story became the basis for the movie Glory.

chusetts Turnpike (I-90) to the Copley Square exit. At the end of the exit, go straight two blocks to Berkeley Street, then take a right onto Boylston Street, which runs directly to the Common.

From the south, take the Southeast Expressway (I-93) to the Massachusetts Avenue exit. Take a right at the end of the exit and follow Massachusetts Avenue to Boylston Street. Go right onto Boylston Street, which runs directly to the Common.

Parking: Parking is available underneath the Common. The entrance to the parking garage is on Charles Street.

The Public Garden

The prettiest and most fragrant spot in central Boston started out as one of the vilest and most foul-smelling. The 25-acre square that would become America's first public botanical garden was originally a stagnant tidal flat, a virtual sewer. Its conversion is a credit to the stubbornness of amateur horticulturalists, the Victorian-era garden movement, and the longstanding rivalry between Boston and New York City.

At first, Round Marsh, as this area was called by Boston's earliest settlers, was simply the shallow shoreline of the Charles River on the western boundary of the Boston Common. During high tide, it was underwater; at low tide, it was a popular place for fishing and clamming. It was from here, at a high point known as Fox Hill, that British troops left in boats for the battles of Lexington and Concord; the exact spot of that historic event is near the Charles Street entrance gate.

Then in 1821, a dam was built by an enterprising businessman to furnish waterpower for his mill. Along the top ran Beacon Street, a narrow causeway with water on both sides, connecting Beacon Hill to Brookline. The unintended effect of this was to prevent the tide from flushing out the water on the inland side of Beacon Street, which became a landlocked swamp. Residents, fed up with the awful smell, successfully petitioned the city to fill in the whole mess.

Problem was, no one could decide what to do with it after that. The City Council called a general meeting to discuss the problem, which gave way to the appointment of an advisory committee. Conscious of the neighborhood's increasing crowding, committee members recommended that the land remain "open for circulation of air from the west for the sake of the health of the

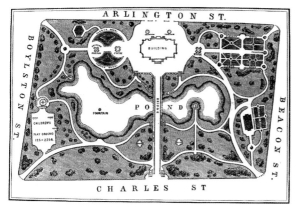

A plan for the Public Garden by Boston architect George F. Meacham was selected in 1859 by the City Council. The plan originally set aside land for a city hall, a playground and a greenhouse, none of which were ever realized.

citizens." They also reached an interesting conclusion: Because the newly reclaimed land was immediately adjacent to the Boston Common, it should be subject to the same immutable restrictions on development.

While the city fathers pondered this interpretation, the land sat unsold and unused, in little better condition than when it was a smelly tidal flat. Then, in 1838, a group of private flower enthusiasts calling themselves the Proprietors of the Botanic Garden in Boston, stepped forward and suggested that a garden be allowed there. Their founder was a wealthy iron manufacturer and amateur gardener named Horace Gray, who had his own greenhouses in Brighton.

The Garden Succeeds . . .

Their proposal accepted, the proprietors engaged an English landscape architect named John Cadness, converted an old circus building into a combination aviary and conservatory, and created the first public botanical garden in the United States. It was a huge success. Here, around 1840, would be shown the first tulips ever displayed in America. Eighty species of birds filled the aviary and the surrounding grounds. Prominent citizens were devoted supporters. At an exhibition of the Massachusetts Horticultural Society held in the garden, Daniel Webster won first prize for a display of vegetables. Ralph Waldo Emerson and Oliver Wendell Holmes liked to meet there for long walks and discussions.

. . . And Falters

But by 1847, the conservatory had burned to the ground, Horace Gray was broke, and the city, under growing pressure to generate property tax revenue, was considering several proposals to develop the site. One called for an enormous Massachusetts Conservancy of Art, Science, and Public Relics; another, for residential housing. In 1850, the City Council formally ruled that the garden site was not a part of Boston Common and recommended housing be allowed. In 1852, it took back the land from what was left of Gray's little band of enthusiasts.

Fortune intervened again, however, when a dispute over property rights delayed any further action for four years, giving backers time to mount a defense of the garden.

This somewhat idealized view of the Public Garden, seen from the steeple of the Arlington Street Church in 1873, looks east towards the domed state capitol off in the distance. By this time many of the trees planted on the Boston Common were beginning to block out the surrounding buildings.

In May of 1904,
E. Chickering & Co.
produced a series of
panoramic photos
that documented
scenes within the
Public Garden

Above, the equestrian
statue of George
Washington is seen
silhouetted against a
skyline not yet domi-
nated by buildings.
Right, forerunners of
the famed Swan Boats
ply the lagoon. Below,
visitors seem more
enamored with the
photographer than
with the budding
spring greenery.

By 1856, they were strong enough to get a referendum on the ballot to prohibit any buildings at the site, except a city hall or structures required for horticultural purposes. The referendum was approved by a margin of sixty to one.

By then, New York was already at work on Central Park, fanning the flames of envy back in Boston. The public parks movement of the 19th century was well under way. Work on the public garden began immediately and with new conviction. The area was finally filled all the way to street level. A design competition was held, with a prize that totaled all of $100; it was won by architect George Meacham, who proceeded to lay out the grounds.

The Garden Reblooms

By 1861, Meecham's centerpiece, a four-acre lagoon modeled after the Serpentine in London's Hyde Park, was providing Bostonians with a tranquil retreat from the city's cares. The Public Garden today still looks almost exactly as Meacham designed it, though a peninsula in the original lagoon was cut off and

made into an island in 1880 after city leaders were shocked to learn that it was being used for lovers' trysts. There continues to be ice skating on the water in the coldest months of winter. The only other thing in Meacham's plans that changed was his idea to build a new city hall at the site where the George Washington statue now stands. The city chose instead to build on School Street.

Bostonians who had worked so hard to save the Public Garden also offered their opinions on every decision—including what plant species should be installed there. In the Victorian era, tropical palms, yucca, and cactus were grown indoors and planted in the garden every summer for exotic effect; they became known as Boston palms. An iron fence was built around the garden in 1865 and restored in 1978 to the original design.

Nor has the passion for this space subsided. When five giant office towers were proposed across the street, 23 civic groups opposed them because their shadows would have crossed the garden. The height of the development was lowered.

A bronze statue of Edward Everett Hale, grand nephew of Revolutionary patriot Nathan Hale and former chaplain of the U. S. Senate, surveys the Public Garden from its Charles Street Gate location. Left, weeping willows and Back Bay buildings frame the garden's lagoon.

A Walking Tour of the Public Garden

If the Boston Common is the anchor of the Emerald Necklace, the Public Garden is the jewel. Bounded by Boylston, Charles, Beacon, and Arlington streets, Boston's Public Garden remains one of its most precious public spaces—with more than 80 species of plants and flowers and 125 kinds of trees, the famous pedal-powered Swan Boats, the world's smallest suspension bridge, one of the finest equestrian statues in America, and a monument to the invention of anesthesia that ingeniously sidesteps the controversy over who discovered it.

Begin your visit at the Charles Street entrance. It was from here on the night of April 18, 1775, that the British left by boat for the battles of Lexington and Concord. Above the entrance is a small oval bas-relief of the town of Boston as it looked around then. The main path through the Garden from Charles Street to Arlington Street is called Haffenreffer Walk after Theodore Haffenreffer, who was a member of the board of park commissioners for

26 years until his death at 76 in 1956.

Just inside the gate are grand red oaks with their spreading branches, named after the color of their leaves in the fall. To the immediate right is a statue of Edward Everett Hale, Civil War–era Unitarian minister and the author of "The Man Without a Country." The bearded Hale is shown in bronze with his hat in one hand and his other on a cane, as if he too was about to take a stroll around the grounds. The statue, by the sculptor Bela Lyon Pratt, was unveiled in 1913. To the reverend's right is a notable linden tree, with a thick rounded crown and fragrant flowers that hang in long-stalked clusters when they bloom in late June and the beginning of July.

To the left of the walk is a memorial to Marvin Goody, an architect and chairman of the Boston Art Commission who was an outspoken defender of the Public Garden. It consists of marble benches around a grand wooden flagpole set in a bronze base designed by A. E. Austin in 1922. Two Norway maples cast their shade over the little plaza—smooth-barked rounded trees with leaves so thick that grass can't grow beneath them.

Monument Row

From here follow the path to the Boylston Street side, where there stands a line of Belgian and English elms interspersed with an occasional maple, and a row of statues peering into the windows of the Four Seasons Hotel across the street. First comes a bronze by Lincoln Memorial sculptor Daniel Chester French of Wendell Phillips, a lawyer who became an ardent abolitionist. Phillips served as president of the American Anti-Slavery Society and

Polish-born Tadeusz Kosciuszko is honored for his Revolutionary-era service to America in its pursuit of freedom from English rule.

also worked for women's suffrage, prison reform, labor reform, and prohibition. He is depicted with one fist clenched against a podium, a link of broken chain held in his other hand. "Prophet of liberty, champion of the slave," reads the inscription.

Between Phillips and the next statue, which memorializes Civil War colonel Thomas Cass, is a proud silver maple, a huge tree that can grow to 100 feet, with five-lobed leaves. Cass commanded the Massachusetts 9th Infantry, known as the Fighting Ninth, which was made up entirely of Irish immigrants. He died in battle at Malvern, Virginia, on July 1, 1862. This work, by sculptor Richard Brooks, won Brooks a gold medal at the Paris Exposition of 1900.

Kosciuszko Memorial

Beside Cass stands a foreign-born hero of another war, the Revolution: Tadeusz Kosciuszko, a Pole who joined the American cause and became a colonel of artillery and George Washington's adjutant. This statue, by Theo Alice Ruggles Kitson, was commissioned by Polish-Americans to commemorate the 150th anniversary of the date Kosciuszko joined the Continental Army in August 1776. The document in his hands is the plan for the fortification of New York's West Point, which Washington had called "the key to America." Kosciuszko supervised

WHETHER IN CHAINS OR IN LAURELS
LIBERTY KNOWS NOTHING BUT VICTORIES

WENDELL PHILLIPS
1811–1884
PROPHET OF LIBERTY
CHAMPION OF THE SLAVE

Abolitionist Wendell Phillips argued that the government owed blacks not merely their freedom, but land, education, and full civil rights as well.

the construction of interlocking batteries, and designed a massive 60-ton chain that prevented the British from advancing north past West Point up the Hudson River.

Next in the queue is Charles Sumner, an antislavery U.S. Senator whose speech against the Missouri Compromise of 1850 lasted two days and, when transcribed, filled 112 pages. He did not mince words, calling opponent Stephen Douglas of Illinois a "noisome, squat, and nameless animal . . . not a proper model for an American senator" and using sexual imagery to insult the absent Andrew Butler of South Carolina. In retaliation, Butler's fellow South Carolinian, Congressman Preston Brooks, rushed in from the House of Representatives and thoroughly bashed Sumner on the head with his gold-topped cane. Sumner became a hero of the North, Brooks of the South. It took Sumner three years to recover from the caning, during which time he was reelected by his defiant state, his empty seat in the Senate chamber speaking for him. Fairness had its limits, however; the first sculptor to submit a design for this statue, Anne Whitney, was rejected because she was a woman, and the commission went to Thomas Ball.

Channing Memorial

At the next corner is a massive statue with its back facing inside the garden and its front facing the Arlington Street Church. This is the Reverend William Ellery Channing, the popular pastor of that church when it was called the Federal Street Church. Channing began his career as a Congregationalist, but adopted what came to be known as Unitarianism and organized the American Unitarian Association. He was also an outspoken abolitionist. "He breathed into theology a

humane spirit and proclaimed anew the divinity of man," reads the inscription on this monument, by sculptor Herbert Adams.

Walk back toward the lagoon. Straight ahead is a weeping willow, its branches drooping toward the surface. Five of these picturesque willows ring the waterway. Follow the banks of the lagoon back toward Charles Street and you'll see three of them. Just past the second is another notable tree, a bald cypress (also called a southern cypress) which, with its thin, feathery leaves and tall, pointed shape, resembles the flame of a match.

A Literary Fountain

Where the lagoon trail nears Haffenreffer Walk again is one of two small fountains that straddle the path at this side of the lagoon. The fountains have identical basins designed in 1861 by Ebenezer Johnson. The statues inside were added in the 1980s. This one, closest to the Swan Boat dock, is one of two works in the park inspired by literature, in this case Rudyard Kipling's *The Jungle Book*. (The other is *Make Way for Ducklings*, coming up later in our tour). Called *Bagheera* after the panther in the Kipling stories, it shows a panther reaching up to

swipe a bird. The statue was designed in 1986 by Lilian Swann Saarinen, wife of the architect Eero Saarinen, who lived in Cambridge.

Swan Boats

From this landing depart the famous seasonal Swan Boats, longtime favorites of parkgoers. The pedal-powered boats, which go two miles an hour, have been operated since 1877 by the family of Robert Paget, an English immigrant and ship-builder who rented out small row-boats on the lagoon. Paget added pedals and later shaped his boats to look like swans.

There are alternating explanations for this fancy. One has it that Paget was inspired by the Wagnerian opera *Lohengrin*, in which the hero crosses a river in a boat drawn by a swan. The other says he used as his models the swans that were import-ed for the lagoon in 1868. Either way, he never had a chance to set the record straight, dying the year after the swan boats first debuted, but his descendants have carried on the tra-dition. For their part, the living swans were removed in the 1960s, but returned to the lagoon in 1991 thanks to the intervention and financial support of a local hotelier.

Cross the Haffenreffer Walk for now and follow the path inside the Charles Street fence to Beacon Street. Here are some of the most interesting trees. First, along Charles Street between the trail and the driveway to the gardeners' storage

trees in this park: a giant redwood, or sequoia, tree. This type of tree boasts the largest trunk girth of any coniferous tree in the world. Its trunk can grow to a diameter of 30 feet, and to a height of 250 feet. Pinelike, the redwood has needle-shaped bluish-green leaves. There is also a dawn redwood, or metasequoia, in this park—distinctive for its sinewy red-colored trunk and puny branches—on the Boylston Street side of the Washington statue. Believed to be extinct, this kind of tree had been seen only in fossils until it was found living in a remote province of China in 1946. There is also a metasequoia in the Arnold Arboretum.

Make Way for Ducklings

If you see the bustle of children, you've found this park's most popular public statue: the duckling sculpture by Nancy Schön. The string of winsome ducks was inspired by the award-winning book by Maine author Robert McCloskey about a family of ducks that gets lost on its way to the Public Garden and is helped across the busy city streets by a policeman. The child-size bronze likenesses of Mr. and Mrs. Mallard waddle their way across the ground beneath a friendly maple, followed closely by Jack, Kack, Lack, Mack, Nack, Ouack, Pack, and Quack. In the summer, the Historic Neighborhoods Foundation runs walking tours following the route of

shed, is a weeping pagoda tree, a round-topped tree with yellowish flowers that bloom brilliantly in the summer. Where the path and the driveway from the little shed converge is a huge European beech, 100 feet tall, with leaves that turn to gold in the fall and a wide trunk into which generations of lovers have carved their initials. Each of the five branches is itself as thick as a tree. Standing in its shadow just across the path is a little-leaf linden, and beside that one of the most exotic

A bronze Jack, Kack, Lack, Mack, Nack, Ouack, Pack, and Quack follow Mrs. Mallard on a never-ending waddle across the Public Garden. Inspired by the book Make Way for Ducklings, *sculptor Nancy Schön created a landmark beloved by young and old alike.*

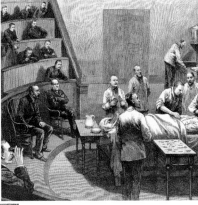

Atop the Ether Monument, sculptor John Quincy Adams Ward portrayed the Good Samaritan comforting a child to commemorate the discovery of ether and its first application at the Massachusetts General Hospital.

Mr. and Mrs. Mallard and their ducklings, ending at the statues—call 617-426-1885 or visit online at www.historic-neighborhoods.org. Boston Park Rangers periodically read from the book here. For Park Ranger program information, call 617-635-4505.

Walk in the direction opposite the ducklings to the corner of Charles and Beacon streets. There you'll find a rare tea crab, a striking vase-shaped tree with small red to yellow fruit and delicate white flowers. Next along is a Japanese tree lilac, a much larger incarnation of a lilac bush, with creamy white flowers that continue to bloom well after other shrub-type lilacs fade. Beside the lilac tree is a Kentucky coffee tree, a potential giant that can reach a height of 100 feet. Its short trunk branches into contorted limbs and twigs. (There is also a Kentucky coffee tree in the Arnold Arboretum.)

The next big tree inside the fence is a silk tree, a member of the legume or pea family, whose seedpods look like pea pods. This tree produces colorful white, pink, and yellow flower clusters from early July into the first weeks of September. Beyond it is a star magnolia, a full-grown version of a tree often stunted so it can be shaped into miniature bonsai plantings. The star magnolia is a slow-growing, bushy shrub that can take as long as 30 years to flower for the first time. When it does, it blooms with white, star-shaped blossoms as much as five inches across sprouting from its bare branches.

Continue to the end of this path. Just inside the corner of Beacon and Arlington streets is the 1924 memo-

Spring bursts forth at the Garden as Kwanzan cherry trees come into blossom. The 25-acre square is home to 40 different species of trees including a rare Camperdown elm, a weeping pagoda tree, and a giant redwood.

rial to George Robert White, the second of the two works in the Public Garden by Daniel Chester French. An angel casting bread upon the waters, the memorial commemorates the philanthropy of White, who made his fortune in the wholesale drug business and left the city $5 million for clinics and for public art—including $50,000 for this memorial to himself. A vast horse chestnut tree shades this corner of the park.

The Ether Monument

Walk back paralleling Arlington Street to the Ether Monument, one of the Garden's more unusual because of the story behind it. Ether was first used successfully as an anesthetic in Boston's Massachusetts General Hospital on October 16, 1846, in an operation to remove a tumor from a patient's neck. Thus ended an era in which people were as likely to die from pain as from any other complications from surgery. A dentist, William T. G. Morton, conducted the operation, assisted by physician Charles T. Jackson, who actually administered the ether. But there was, and remains, a controversy over which man deserved the credit. Sculptor John Quincy Adams Ward sidestepped the question by neither naming nor depicting either man. Instead he erected a tall pedestal with lion heads at its base, at the top of which he portrayed the Good Samaritan supporting and comforting a child. The monument, said Oliver Wendell Holmes, is "to ether—or either." (At least four other men beside Morton and Jackson also claimed to have discovered ether.) Beside the monument stands a huge ginkgo boloba, or maidenhair tree, from China, looking for all the world like the talking trees of Oz with its thick, dark stalk, and armlike branches. And between the Ether Monument and the Beacon Street fence is one of the most important trees here: a pagoda tree considered one of the finest in the country. Its lacy spread of tiny, colorful flowers sprout from a trunk that seems to be twisting up from the ground into its myriad branches.

The Washington Statue

Turn around and head toward the George Washington statue near the Arlington Street entrance. On the way, to the left of the path, are two Kwanzan cherry trees like those

whose bloom turns Washington D.C. pink each April. These vase-shape trees with shiny bark sprout double blossoms.

Here the landscape opens into flower beds, often planted with colorful tulips but rotated year-round with flowers from the city's greenhouses in Franklin Park. Even the Victorian-era conceit of planting tropical palms has been resumed, to great effect, and there are also carefully sculpted hedges. In the center: the huge 1869 statue by Thomas Ball of George Washington astride his horse, considered one of the finest equestrian statues in the country (though Washington's sword has been broken so often that it has been replaced with fiberglass, which is cheaper to replace).

Ball's small plaster study of this statue is in the Boston Athenaeum. He reportedly studied horses in local stables for four years to get the anatomy of this one just right. His only lapse: he forgot to give it a tongue.

Now we can take the leisurely stroll down Haffenreffer Walk and

The world's shortest suspension bridge, erected in 1867, allows visitors to cross the lagoon at its narrowest point.

back toward the Charles Street Gate, across Meacham's lagoon, designed to resemble the Serpentine in London's Hyde Park. One thing Boston has that London doesn't is the world's smallest suspension bridge, designed by William G. Preston and built in 1867 to carry this path across the thinnest point of the lagoon. (The bridge has since been reinforced from below, and the cables are now only decorative.) The Japanese lantern in the lagoon to the left is from the palace of Toyotomi Hideyoshi, a 16th-century Japanese general, given as a gift in 1905 and restored in 1993.

The Public Garden is open from 6 a.m. until 11:30 p.m., though foot traffic continues at all hours.

The Public Garden is bordered by Boylston, Charles, Beacon, and Arlington streets. For information about public ice skating on the lagoon, call 617-635-4505. The Swan Boats operate in the spring, summer, and fall. For information, call 617-522-1966.

How to Get to the Public Garden

By subway: Take the MBTA Green Line to Arlington Street.

By car: From Cambridge, take Memorial Drive to the Longfellow Bridge over the Charles River. At the end of the bridge, take a right onto Charles Street,

which runs directly to the Public Garden.

From the west, take the Massachusetts Turnpike (I-90) to the Copley Square exit. At the end of the exit, go straight two blocks to Berkeley Street, then take a right onto Boylston Street, which runs directly to the Public Garden.

From the south, take the Southeast Expressway (I-93) to the Massachusetts Avenue exit. Take a right at the end of the exit and follow Massachusetts Avenue to Boylston Street. Go right onto Boylston Street, which runs directly to the Public Garden.

Parking: Parking is available underneath the Boston Common. The entrance to the parking garage is on Charles Street.

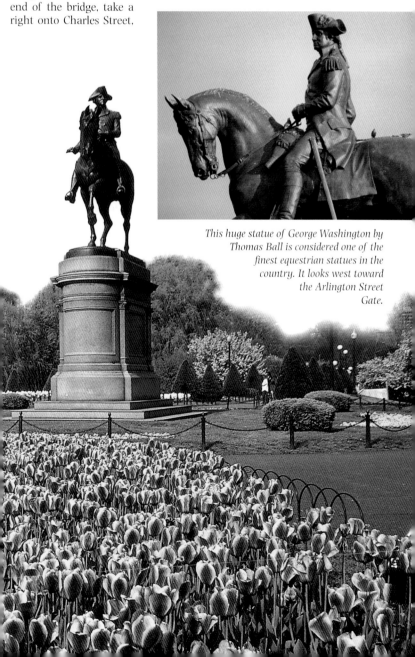

This huge statue of George Washington by Thomas Ball is considered one of the finest equestrian statues in the country. It looks west toward the Arlington Street Gate.

The Commonwealth Avenue Mall

Commonwealth Avenue was designed to be Boston's grandest boulevard. For that matter, in a city that grew randomly over narrow cow paths and along the uneven contours of its original peninsula, Commonwealth Avenue and its parallel streets were the first to be formally planned at all. Built on landfill and laid out in even squares, they would almost instantly become the city's most illustrious addresses.

In the second part of the 19th century, by contrast, "Back Bay" was synonymous with "open cesspool." The Roxbury and Boston Mill Company dam had blocked the tidal currents from carrying away the city's sewage, which accumulated into what became a fetid swamp. Not even the earlier filling of the Public Garden had helped.

In 1858, the state took control of the bay and began to fill it in, running trains day and night with gravel from the hilly suburban town of Needham. Ultimately, 450 acres of new land would be created over 30 years, enlarging the size of the city by nearly 60 percent and molding Boston into something like its present shape. There would be plenty of room for open spaces in this part of town—and Commonwealth Avenue would be the centerpiece.

A design competition was held. Architect Arthur Gilman submitted the winning plan, a broad Parisian-style boulevard with a 100-foot-wide green space down the middle. (The road is 220 feet wide from stoop to stoop). Bostonians loved it. Work on the street began in 1856 and,

before long, the state was selling the land for three times what it cost to fill it in. Boston's wealthiest residents competed to build mansions for themselves along this stylish new avenue with its formal central promenade shaded by two rows of elm trees. It was to be a cityscape appropriate to the city's golden age of intellect and commerce.

When the Emerald Necklace was conceived, Bostonians exhibited

A leisurely stroll down the mall under sheltering elm trees evokes a 19th century pace marred only by the cars parked in front of the historic Commonwealth Avenue mansions.

another of their famous characteristics: Yankee thrift. Reasoning that it was cheaper to lay out its string of parks along land that was already publicly owned, it consolidated the Commonwealth Avenue Mall into the scheme.

Commonwealth Avenue remains a prestigious address. Although many of the mansions have been subdivided into condominiums and apartments in a city hungry for housing, on the outside they look much the same. There has been one other dramatic change: Along the mall, Gilmore's elms have long since died, replaced by sweetgum, green ash, maple, linden, dogwood, mag-

A panoramic photo, c. 1903, showing the mall down Commonwealth Avenue. The building at the far left is the Algonquin Club, designed in the then popular Classical Revival style by McKim, Mead & White in 1887. The club was started by Boston Globe founder Charles H. Taylor because he knew his Brahmin betters would never admit him to their own club, the Somerset.

nolia, and Japanese pagoda trees. In early May, the magnolia and dogwood trees erupt in pink blooms.

A Walking Tour of the Mall

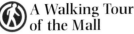

The Commonwealth Avenue Mall begins where the Public Garden ends, at the Garden's Arlington Street Gate. This part of the city is laid out on a grid, and the cross streets go in alphabetical order beginning with Arlington, followed by Berkeley, Clarendon, Dartmouth, Exeter, Fairfield, Gloucester, and Hereford. Parallel with Commonwealth to the left is Newbury Street, the city's swankiest shopping district; to the right is Marlborough Street, one of its quietest residential neighborhoods. Parallel to them are Boylston and Beacon streets, respectively.

The entrance to the mall is modest: granite posts and cast-iron ornamental fences flank the passage from the Public Garden to the footpath on the mall. There is a pair of simple stone benches just inside the gate, one commemorating Union veterans of the Civil War and one remembering Charles Pagelson Howard, a lawyer who helped preserve this stretch of green space in the 1950s and 1960s. But the ambience is grand, thanks to the Victorian-era mansions that begin here and continue virtually uninterrupted on both sides. The residential homes went up one after another on this stretch of the road from 1861 until 1870, each owner and architect trying to outdo the last.

Alexander Hamilton

The first in the eclectic succession of luminaries memorialized along the mall is Alexander Hamilton, private secretary to General George

Washington's famous crossing of the Delaware owes its place in history to Revolutionary War general John Glover, commander of the regiment of Marblehead fishermen who ferried him across.

Washington and first U.S. Secretary of the Treasury, who later schemed against political enemies including President John Adams and Aaron Burr; Hamilton would die in a duel with Burr in 1804. The sculptor of this granite statue is almost as interesting as its subject: William Rimmer, a self-taught medical doctor whose father believed himself to be Louis XVII, the lost dauphin of France.

General John Glover

Much of the ornamental wrought-iron fencing that once graced the mall is gone, but some was replaced in 1987, including both sides of Berkeley Street. Beyond the fence, on the block of the mall between Berkeley and Clarendon streets, stands General John Glover, commander of the Revolutionary War regiment of Marblehead fishermen who ferried the American army across the Delaware on December 25, 1776, to rout the unsuspecting Hessians in the Battle of Trenton.

A moving tribute in bronze and marble commemorates the nine firemen who died fighting a blaze at the nearby Hotel Vendome in 1972.

William Lloyd Garrison sits imposingly at his Commonwealth Avenue site. An ardent abolitionist and publisher of The Liberator, *he went so far as to advocate Northern secession from the Union because the Constitution permitted slavery.*

The owner of his own fishing fleet, Glover contributed his entire considerable fortune into the war effort. Though he rose to the rank of brigadier general in 1777, he was reduced after the war to working as a shoemaker. The 1875 statue is the work of Martin Milmore, famous for the Roxbury Soldiers Monument at Forest Hills Cemetery and the Soldiers and Sailors Monument on Boston Common.

Patrick Andrew Collins

Towering over the brownstones to the left are Boston's tallest buildings, the John Hancock Tower and the Prudential Tower. And next along the mall is a man who briefly ran the city before it sprouted high-rise landmarks like these. Patrick Andrew Collins rose from his beginnings as an Irish immigrant upholsterer to become a lawyer, state legislator, Congressman, and U.S. consul general to London. Elected mayor of Boston in 1902, Collins died in office only three years later. His bearded bust stands on a high tier between metaphorical figures representing America and Ireland. Collins was born in Ireland, the inscription notes, and "was always her lover." The statue, by Theo Alice Ruggles Kitson (whose work includes the Tadeusz Kosciuszko memorial in the Public Garden) and her husband, Henry Hudson Kitson (sculptor of the Minuteman statue on Lexington Common), was moved to this spot from Kenmore Square in 1968.

Vendome Fire Memorial

On the same stretch of the mall is its newest monument, this one a memorial to nine firemen who died fighting a blaze at the Hotel Vendome on June 17, 1972. Their names, and a chronology of the fire, are chiseled into black marble over which is draped a firefighter's jacket and a fire helmet made of bronze. The Vendome, which was rebuilt, stands on the left on the next block.

William Lloyd Garrison

Next is a statue of a seated William Lloyd Garrison, one of the leaders of the abolitionist movement and publisher of the antislavery newspaper *The Liberator*, a copy of which he holds in his hand. A pacifist, Garrison thought the North should secede from the South. This work is by Olin Levi Warner.

Samuel Eliot Morison

The most popular sculpture on the mall is the one that follows Garrison's: the 1982 bronze of Admiral (in the U.S. Naval Reserves) Samuel Eliot Morison sitting on the shore wearing a fisherman's oilskins and cap and staring out to sea, a pair of binoculars in one hand. SAILOR-HISTORIAN it says. Morison was a Harvard professor and Pulitzer prizewinning maritime historian who personally retraced the route of Christopher Columbus in a sailboat and also wrote two Pulitzer prizewinning biographies. He was a member of the St. Botolph Club just across the street on the right. Morison died in 1976. His statue, by sculptor Penelope Jencks, was commissioned by the Back Bay Federation. Ivy grows like barnacles on the base, and passages from Morison's writings are inscribed on the surrounding rocks. When it rains, water pours down the collar of his oilskins.

Domingo Sarmiento

The stocky figure of Domingo Sarmiento is next. Sarmiento, a president of Argentina, was determined worthy of a place here because he based his nation's educational system on the model proposed by Horace Mann, the first Massachusetts education commissioner. A gift of Argentina, the statue was the work of Argentinian sculptor Ivette Compagnion.

Here the road dips under Massachusetts Avenue, and the mall halts, re-emerging on the other side. It's one of several 20th-century changes made to accommodate automobile traffic that have foiled the original idea of a continuous and uninterrupted chain of parks. Pedestrians have to cross to the sidewalk, cross Massachusetts Avenue, then cross again to see the last in the series of statues on the mall. The bridge itself that carries Massachusetts Avenue above the road is named for Tommy Leonard, bartender at the former Eliot Lounge in the Eliot Hotel, which sits on the corner of Commonwealth and Massachusetts avenues. The Eliot

was the unofficial clubhouse of Boston's many runners, and a shrine to visitors who came to compete in the Boston Marathon, whose route briefly follows Commonwealth Avenue. Closed in 1996, the Eliot Lounge has been replaced by an upscale restaurant.

Leif Eriksson

At the orphaned end of the mall is a presence even odder than that of the president of Argentina. It's a statue whose subject is often mistaken for a woman thanks to the prominent armored breastplates, a confusion hardly lessened by the fact that the inscription is in Runic, the language of the ancient Vikings. In fact, this is supposed to be the Viking explorer Leif Eriksson, and he's here because a Harvard chemistry professor concluded after a lifetime of study that Vikings under the command of Eriksson's brother Thorwald not only brought their longboats into Boston Harbor six centuries before the Pilgrims, but rowed them up the Charles River as far as a place called Norumbega. Professor Ebon Norton Horsford, who was independently wealthy, personally paid for this statue by Anne Whitney—the same sculptor who was turned down for the job of depicting Charles Sumner in the Public Garden—and for a tower at the presumed site of the Norumbega settlement, which Horsford calculated was in modern-day Weston. Bas-relief plaques on the monument show Thorwald climbing ashore from a longboat; Leif Eriksson was meant to be staring out to sea, but his gaze today is in the general direction of the Fenway Park scoreboard.

The Commonwealth Avenue Mall is open from 6 a.m. until 11:30 p.m., though foot traffic continues at all hours.

How to Get to the Mall

By subway: Take the MBTA Green Line to the Arlington Street, Copley Square, Massachusetts Avenue, or Kenmore stations, or Bus 1 from Dudley Square or Central Square to Commonwealth Avenue.

By car: From Cambridge, take Memorial Drive to the John Harvard Bridge, which carries Massachusetts Avenue over the Charles River. Commonwealth Avenue is the third street on the Boston side.

From the west, take the Massachusetts Turnpike (I-90) to the Prudential Center exit. At the

end of the exit, go straight to Massachusetts Avenue. Take a right on Massachusetts Avenue and follow Massachusetts Avenue to Commonwealth Avenue.

From the south, take the Southeast Expressway (I-93) to the Massachusetts Avenue exit. Take a right at the end of the exit and follow Massachusetts Avenue to Commonwealth Avenue.

Parking on Commonwealth Avenue is by resident permit only,

After winning his first Pulitzer Prize in 1942, Harvard professor Samuel Eliot Morison was commissioned by President Franklin Delano Roosevelt to write a history of U.S. naval operations in World War II and given the rank of lieutenant commander.

though there are metered spaces on most cross streets and on Newbury and Boylston streets. Parking is also available underneath the Boston Common. The entrance to the parking garage is on Charles Street.

The Back Bay Fens

No sooner had Boston's denizens moved to their grand new mansions on the Commonwealth Avenue Mall than they started to complain about the smell. Filling in this section of the Back Bay had not solved the problem of raw sewage baking on the Charles River tidal flats. It had only pushed it farther away and concentrated it into a single flood-prone tidal salt marsh fed by the polluted Stony Brook and the aptly named, sluggish Muddy River. "Citizens of Boston," one reader wrote to the Boston *Daily Advertiser.* "Have you ever visited the Mall; have you ever inhaled the Western breeze, fragrant with perfume, refreshing every sense and invigorating every nerve? What think you of converting the [Back Bay] water which skirts the Common into an empty Mud Basin, reeking with filth, abhorrent to the smell, and disgusting to the eye? By every god of sea, lake, or fountain, it is incredible." Meanwhile, no matter how repellent was this swamp, the shortage of available land for housing forced the city's newest, poorest immigrants to live in tenements beside it. Typhoid and other diseases started running rampant.

Despite the increasing overcrowding, there remained a critical scarcity of public open space. By 1875, Boston still had only 115 acres of parks, of which the Boston Common and the Public Garden comprised more than half. New York's Central Park and Prospect Park alone were a combined 1,300 acres.

Enter Olmsted

A parks commission was approved by referendum in 1875, and set out to solve at least the second of these two problems by filling in the tidal basin on the Charles. It held a design competition and awarded $500 for the winning plans to a man named Herman Grundel. But Frederick Law Olmsted, who, as mentioned previously, had been keeping a close eye on park plans, pointed out that Grundel's scheme failed completely to deal with the sewage situation. The parks commission sent Grundel away with his cash prize—and hired Olmsted.

The 150-acre natural setting Olmsted created from this fetid tidal swamp would cleverly conceal a major work of drainage and engineering. He built a tidal gate where the marsh connected with the Charles to control the water level, and a series of man-made rivers and ponds to hold the overflow from heavy rains. During heavy rains, the low points of the park itself would serve as temporary holding basins, preventing the runoff from affecting the surrounding streets and buildings. The trees and shrubs that Olmsted planted were chosen to withstand these sudden periodic influxes of water. And the name he selected for his new 150-acre park was the Fens, named after the marsh-

It took Frederick Law Olmsted's men 10 years of continuous dredging with steam-operated shovels on barges to rid what eventually became the Back Bay Fens of the "Mud Basin, reeking with filth, abhorrent to the smell, and disgusting to the eye."

In his solution for the Boylston Street Bridge, consulting architect H. H. Richardson clearly answered Olmsted's wish for a bridge that would "have a rustic quality and be picturesque in material as well as in outlines and shadows."

lands or "fens" of eastern England.

It took 10 years just to dredge the area, beginning in 1880. Stony Brook and the Muddy River were rerouted through the middle. Olmsted planned "a fenny verdure, [with] meandering water and blooming islets." He described a scene of "a winding brackish creek within wooded banks, gaining interest from the meandering course of the water [with] numerous points and coves softened in their outlines by thickets and with much delicate variety in tone and color" and with "picturesque elements emphasized by a few necessary structures."

Plans Go Awry

When the Back Bay Fens was opened, the same Commonwealth Avenue elite that had literally held their noses at the area rushed to use the park. It became a popular place to promenade, attracting horseback riders and ladies in carriages along a network of bridle paths Olmsted called the Ride. It drew canoeists to the narrow winding rivers. And it sparked the development of museums, colleges, apartment buildings—and, in 1912, Fenway Park, where the Red Sox still play. One of the city's most extravagant socialites, Elizabeth Stewart Gardner, even took the town by surprise by moving from Beacon Street and building a mansion along the Fenway in the style of a 15th-century Venetian palace.

But Olmsted's first major Boston park has not been a complete success. The drainage system turned out to be flawed from the outset, and the Charles itself had to be dammed in 1910, transforming salt water to freshwater. That killed off many of Olmsted's original plantings and attracted a scourge of dense-growing reeds that continues to this day. The layout of the park was also changed. Playing fields were added in 1912, and stadium seats built on the sloping lawns. The entire park was redesigned in the formal landscape style by Olmsted disciple Arthur Shurcliff in the 1920s. The connecting link with Commonwealth Avenue was effectively broken by the construction of the Park Drive overpass from Storrow Drive. And a parking lot was built beside a Sears Roebuck warehouse, cutting off the stretch of green space that connected the Fens with the Riverway, and exacerbating the chronic flooding problems. (The pavement was removed and the green space restored in 1998.) Meanwhile, the sluggish Muddy River was becoming heavily silted. All of these problems culminated in two devastating floods in 1996 and 1998 that inundated roads, buildings, and subway tunnels, causing an estimated $100 million in damage. (New flood-control improvements are now planned.) All that's left of Olmsted's design are two original bridges, the park's general boundaries, and some early trees.

This is not to say the Fens is unpopular. On the contrary; it's one of the busiest places in the Emerald Necklace, bordered as it is by college campuses, popular museums, and apartment houses now occupied largely by students. Its athletic fields are almost constantly in use. And the Boston Athletic Association half marathon begins here. Proceeds go to the Emerald Necklace Conservancy.

A Walking Tour of the Back Bay Fens

The Fens begins the section of the Emerald Necklace that was built from scratch by Frederick Law Olmsted. This chain of open space is linked by narrow tree-lined park-ways, some with grassy medians, designed to maintain the impression that this is an unbroken line.

The Fenway gives way to the Riverway (which for most of its length is both a parkway and a park, following the route of the Muddy River); to the Jamaicaway past Olmsted Park and Jamaica Pond, connecting Jamaica Pond with the Arnold Arboretum; and to the Arborway joining the arboretum with Franklin Park.

The tangle of one-way streets bor-dering the Back Bay Fens looks ele-gant on a map but is almost impossi-ble to navigate in a car, even for vet-eran Bostonians. Although the link was largely severed by the unfortu-nate addition of elevated access ramps from Storrow Drive to Park Drive, it's still possible to walk the short distance from the end of the Commonwealth Avenue Mall to the Back Bay Fens. But among the many other changes made to Olmsted's original plans for this park, the formal entrance was shifted to Westland Avenue in 1905.

Erin is depicted weaving a wreath of laurel and oak for her sons Poetry and Patriotism at the back of the O'Reilly Monument.

Westland Gate

This is a good place to begin—and an excellent vantage point to see how Olmsted's park has changed. The Westland Gate was designed by Guy Lowell, architect of the nearby Museum of Fine Arts. Originally called the Johnson Memorial Foun-tain, it was built in 1905 in memory of a wealthy Bostonian named Jesse Johnson by his wife. Each of the two square pillars flanking the street has four bronze lions near its base; the lions, facing apart, shoot water from their mouths into shallow basins. The gate was restored in 1980, though the fountain seldom oper-ates.

Behind it is not a picturesque scene from nature, as Olmsted planned, but the stark wall of the one-story Beaux Arts–style Boston Fire Department alarm center, which was built in 1927. It's not much of a first impression, and the huge radio antenna and rusting chain-link fence don't help.

Turn right here. Original dog-woods, lindens, hawthornes, and red oaks line this edge of the park. But the dominant vegetation, to say the least, is phragmites (frag-my´-tees), a common reed that grows as high as 15 feet in wet, low-lying places such as this end of the Fens. The thick-growing phragmites, which crowds out other wetland plants,

Memorials to Boston's WW II, Korean, and Vietnam War dead remind visitors of the city's longtime contribution to maintaining America's freedom.

afflicts the park like a weed, and blocks the view from here of the Muddy River.

O'Reilly Memorial

Just ahead, at the busy corner of Boylston and the Fenway is the John Boyle O'Reilly Memorial, sculpted in 1894 by Daniel Chester French to memorialize the Irish poet and editor of the Catholic newspaper *The Pilot*. Accused of treason by the English, O'Reilly was banished to the penal colony in Australia; but he became one of the few convicts to escape there, rescued by the crew of an American ship. His countenance looks out upon the traffic, but behind him and at the rear of the monument is a scene depicting Erin weaving a wreath of laurel and oak for her sons Poetry and Patriotism. The calligraphy on the monument is Celtic.

Follow the sidewalk along the park's edge and over the Boylston Street bridge, one of only two that are original to the Fens. A small platform that bulges outward and away from the path of pedestrians affords a nice view of the park, including that endless sea of reeds along the still languid Muddy River.

Parker Victory Gardens

Take the path to the left at the end of the bridge. This leads quickly to the Richard D. Parker Memorial Victory Gardens, the only World War II vic-

tory garden remaining in Boston, and the largest urban community garden in New England. Laid out here are more than 450 fragrant plots—among them, a garden designed for the disabled, a children's garden, a Japanese garden, and a parcel tended by the Massachusetts Horticultural Society. But most of these tiny patches are cultivated by local amateur gardeners who personalize them not only with exotic vines and flowers, but with trellises, hedges, wooden gates, and lawn ornaments. Birds drawn by the birdbaths and birdhouses sing in the trees, including another of Olmsted's originals: a weeping willow whose drooping branches straddle the path.

Continue to the corner. Across the street to the right are visible the light stanchions and upper grandstands of Fenway Park. Opened with a game against the New York Highlanders (now the Yankees) on April 20, 1912—the week the Titanic sank—the historic ballpark is the oldest in America. Among the greats who played there: Cy Young, Babe Ruth, Joe Cronin, Bobby Doerr, Johnny Pesky, Ted Williams, Carlton Fisk, Jim Rice and Carl Yastrzemski. As any Red Sox fan will grumble, the team won its last World Series at Fenway—in 1918. In fact, the Sox first played under the name of the Boston Pilgrims beginning in 1901, in a ballpark on the other side of the Fens: the Huntington Avenue Grounds, where the first World Series was played in 1903. That time, Boston won. There is a piece of granite shaped like home plate and a statue of Cy Young at the original site, now behind Northeastern University's Cabot Cage.

World War II, Korea, and Vietnam Memorials

With the park on your left, follow the perimeter, crossing Agassiz Road (which simply cuts across to Westland Avenue, where we arrived). Just past this road is one of the more elaborate works of public art in Boston's parks: the city's World War II memorial. It was designed by, again, John Paramino—sculptor of the Marquis de Lafayette, Commodore John Barry, the Declaration of Independence monument, and the Founder's Memorial on Boston Common. Paramino, need it be pointed out, was a great friend of the mayor.

Dedicated in 1949, the World War II memorial shows Victory holding a laurel wreath, wings outstretched, before a square pillar capped with stars and military emblems, and it's backed by an ellipse listing the names of Bostonians lost in the war. It is named for U.S. Army Sergeant Charles A. MacGillivary, a Canadian native and Boston resident who received the Congressional Medal of Honor for singlehandedly disabling five German machine-gun nests near Woelfling, France, on New Year's Day, 1945. Opposite the monument are two smaller memorials added in 1989 to Boston men who died in Korea and Vietnam. This is the quietest section of the park, surrounded by birches and willows.

Kelleher Rose Garden

Behind the memorial, screened by a high hedge, is the James P. Kelleher Rose Garden. Originally part of a 30-acre flood-storage marsh, this site was considered for a huge horticultural greenhouse in 1913, but the project died for lack of funding. In 1921, a "concert grove" was proposed, but the success of a display garden in Franklin Park persuaded planners to instead allow a rose garden. Between 1927 and 1930, a lagoon was created and the area regraded to allow for a circular garden in a design prepared by Arthur Shurcliff. A rectangular addition was later attached. After midcentury neglect, the garden was reopened in 1997 with a high tea hosted by the mayor's wife, which has since become an annual tradition.

The Kelleher is accredited by All-

American Rose Selection (AARS), meaning that it must display "roses that have exhibited superior qualities during at least two years of nationwide testing and judging." Among them are the grandiflora Tournament of Roses, the winner of the AARS's highest rose award in 1989; the 1983 winner, the pink Sweet Surrender; and the 1994 champion, the yellow-to-cream hybrid tea rose Midas Touch. The names of the roses hang from the hedges behind them. At one end of the rectangle is a reproduction of *Desonsol*, a weeping female nude presented by Boston's sister city, Barcelona, and reproduced from the 1911 original in that city by Catalan artist Josep Llimona. And in the center of the oval, which is ringed by trellis-covered paths, is a 325-year-old ceremonial bell from a Japanese religious shrine that was confiscated by the Japanese government as scrap

The Kelleher Rose Garden, established in 1930, contains over 200 varieties of tea, floribunda, and grandiflora hybrids.

metal near the end of World War II. It survived the war intact and was taken home to Boston as a souvenir by sailors on the USS *Boston*. Asked if they wanted it returned, Japanese diplomats replied it should remain as a gesture of world peace.

Beyond this point is the busy athletic area, with a baseball diamond, a softball diamond, a soccer pitch, a running track, and two basketball courts.

Built in 1912, the baseball fields were later named for right fielder Roberto Clemente, who played for the Pittsburgh Pirates, batting .414 in the 1971 World Series. Clemente died in 1972 while flying relief supplies to Nicaraguan earthquake victims. A small memorial to Clemente was created by artist Anthony Forgione in 1976. The stadium seat-

The Roberto Clemente baseball fields were named to honor the ballplayer who died in 1972 while flying relief supplies to Nicaraguan earthquake victims.

The rose was first
brought by colonists to
North America in the
17th century, making it
the longest cultivated
European plant in this
country. Accredited by the AARS, the Kelleher Rose Garden offers the
visitor a glorious display including (from left to right, top to bottom)
All That Jazz, All American Beauty, Impatient, Broadway, Amber Queen,
Shreveport, Camelot, Chicago Peace, Fragrant Cloud, Tiffany, Peace,
Christian Dior, Century, Sheer Elegance, and Betty Boop.

ing, which follows the slope of Olmsted's lawns, was added in 1925.

Beyond the fields, to the right, the park branches off into a narrow strip of grass between two parallel streets, and toward the Riverway. Here, too, the connecting link was broken after Sears Roebuck lobbied successfully to convert it to a parking lot for a regional warehouse in 1928. The long-abandoned art deco–style warehouse was rehabbed into an office and retail complex in 1998 and the link restored, complete with grass and trees.

Continuing the Walk

For now, instead of following this spur, continue along the sidewalk as it rounds the corner, hugging the riverbank at water level. Across the street on the right is Simmons College, one of several educational institutions around the Fens (the others are Emmanuel and Wheelock colleges, the Massachusetts College of Art, the Massachusetts College of Pharmacy, Northeastern, and the Wentworth Institute of Technology).

Next to Simmons is Mrs. Gardner's mansion, now the Elizabeth Stewart Gardner Museum. The museum, which Gardner opened to the public in 1903, surrounds a three-story interior garden courtyard. It features more than 2,500 paintings, sculptures, tapestries, and other objects, with a focus on the Italian Renaissance, including works by Titian, Botticelli, and Raphael; and by Rembrandt, Degas, Matisse, Sargent, and Whistler.

The grand rear façade of the Museum of Fine Arts (MFA) comes up next on the right. Opened in 1876, the museum is one of the world's best, with 350,000 objects from the Americas, Europe, Asia, Oceania (the Pacific), and Africa. There are textiles, furniture, musical instruments, prints, drawings, and photographs. The pair of stone field houses on the left were built in 1928 and are undergoing a long process of renovation.

Across the street from the Fens, beside the MFA and just before we come full circle to our starting point, is a massive statue to the first governor of the Massachusetts Bay Colony, John Endecott, doffing his Pilgrim hat. The stone statue was sculpted in 1937 by C. P. Jennewin, who specialized in Pilgrims; he also created the Pilgrim Mother statue in Plymouth.

Born in England in 1588, Endecott came to Massachusetts in 1628 and was leader of the colony until the arrival of John Winthrop two years later; Endecott also later succeeded Winthrop for several terms as governor. Though he himself came seeking refuge from religious persecution, he was a fierce persecuter of Quakers and other religious dissenters, hanging them on Boston Common.

The Back Bay Fens is open from 6 a.m. until 11:30 p.m. Walking in this park after dark is not recommended.

The Fens is roughly bordered by Park Drive, Boylston Street, and the Fenway.

How to Get to the Fens

By subway: Take the MBTA Green Line "E" train or Bus 39 from Copley Square to Symphony station. Walk north (toward Cambridge) one block to Westland Avenue; Symphony Hall will be on your left. Take a left on Westland and follow it to the entrance on the park. Or take the MBTA Green Line "E" train or Bus 39 from Copley Square to Museum station and circle around to the back of the Museum of Fine Arts. Or take the Green Line "B," "C," or "D" train to the Massachusetts Avenue/Convention Center station. Leave by the Massachusetts Avenue exit and take a left and walk five blocks to Westland Avenue. Take a right on Westland and follow it to the entrance of the park.

By car: From Cambridge, take Memorial Drive to the John Harvard Bridge, which carries Massachusetts Avenue over the Charles River. Follow Massachusetts Avenue to Westland Avenue. Take a right on Westland and follow it to the entrance of the park.

From the west, take the Massachusetts Turnpike (I-90) to the Prudential Center exit. At the end of the exit, go straight to Massachusetts Avenue. Take a right on Massachusetts Avenue, then the first left (Westland Avenue). Follow Westland to the entrance of the park.

From the south, take the Southeast Expressway (I-93) to the Massachusetts Avenue exit. Take a right at the end of the exit and follow Massachusetts Avenue to Westland Avenue. Take a left on Westland and follow it to the entrance of the park.

Parking: Nonresident street parking around the Fens is almost nonex-

istent, but there are metered spaces on Huntington Avenue and Massachusetts Avenue nearby and a parking garage at the Museum of Fine Arts.

The Riverway

A combination of park and parkway, the Riverway is the name of both the busy tree-lined road and the quiet undulating sanctuary running alongside it. A lot is crammed into this narrow strip of land: the Muddy River, several parallel walking and bicycling trails, a stretch of greenway that once served as a bridle path, a rail line, and some of the most impressive (and expensive) bridges in the Emerald Necklace. Meant to mimic a natural New England wetland forest, the Riverway is actually almost completely man-made.

The boundary separating Boston from Brookline, the Muddy River was a stagnant no-man's land by the end of the 19th century, clogged with pollution and lined with dumps and shacks. A park was envisioned there by Frederick Law Olmsted, not only as a solution to the drainage problems but also to connect the Fens with Jamaica Pond, the Arnold Arboretum, and Franklin Park. In a rare show of cooperation, Boston and Brookline agreed in 1890 to jointly undertake the project, which included rerouting the river itself to create a winding stream, and building an embankment along the Brookline side to block the sight of the Boston & Albany Railroad tracks that ran there. The park was also laid out so the adjoining road would run unseen above it on the other side.

The Riverway includes some of the grandest bridges in the city, fore-

Shown under construction, the Riverway section of the Muddy River is on the dividing line between Brookline and Boston.

most among them the Shepley, Rutan & Coolidge–designed bridge that carries Longwood Avenue across it. Successors to H. H. Richardson, Shepley and Coolidge had inherited his practice in 1886, and would go on to design both the Chicago Public Library and the Art Institute of Chicago. Here their commissions included not only the Longwood Avenue bridge and other, similar bridges at the Riverway's Brookline Avenue end, but an extraordinary small stone shelter with a pitched wooden roof—called the Round House—near the Short Street entrance.

Construction of this slender urban woodland attracted elegant apartment buildings along both sides, and later private schools, hospitals now ranked among the world's best, and small colleges including Simmons, Wheelock, and Emmanual. The side streets on the Brookline side are lined with colorful Victorian houses, though the builders of these were drawn as much by the commuter rail line as by the park.

The Riverway remains relatively intact, and some of its structures have been painstakingly restored. The rail tracks today are used by the electric trolleys on the suburban Riverside spur of the Massachusetts Bay Transportation Authority, which disgorge students, teachers, and white-coated medical professionals each day across the grassy woods and granite bridges to the Longwood academic and medical district.

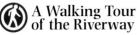 A Walking Tour of the Riverway

A slim band of green space between the MBTA tracks and the parkway of the same name, the Riverway is bounded at its ends by Park Drive and Route 9. It comprises 28 acres in all, but seems larger because of optical illusions created by designer Frederick Law Olmsted. An embankment hides the trolley tracks on one edge, for example, and thick woods (the Boundary Forest) screen the road, which itself is lined on both sides with American lindens. Some of the trees here are among the oldest and the largest in the city's parks, planted at the end of the 19th century.

A Link Restored

As mentioned earlier, the link between the Fens and the Riverway was severed in 1928 when a parking lot was built to serve a Sears Roebuck warehouse, but the connection was restored in 1998. So was the enormous warehouse, which had been abandoned but was renovated into offices, restaurants, and stores and renamed the Landmark Center. Young red maples are sprouting in the reclaimed section of the park.

Enter the Riverway here at the Landmark Center end. The squat brick building near the entrance was built in 1895 as a maintenance facility, and there is still a Boston Parks Department truck yard on the other side. The building itself now houses the Boston Youth Fund.

The Muddy River seems to start from nowhere, but this is actually its end. From here, it flows into an unseen culvert that discharges in the Charles. Two walking paths flank the Muddy River; take the one between the river and the trolley tracks.

Immediately on the left along the water begin the inevitable tenacious phragmites reeds. The path here is shaded from both sides by huge century-old oak trees, some of the tallest in the city, which weave a high, arched canopy of branches overhead. On the left, rare birches overhang the river. Another, smaller path diverges to the right, where there is an old iron bridge whose parts are joined with chubby rivets, a fascinating, if now off-limits vestige of the old Boston & Albany Railroad.

On the left are two of the stone bridges by Shepley, Rutan & Coolidge, one that spans the river and another that seems to arch over nothing at all. In fact, there was once a bridle path beneath this second bridge.

Both of these structures have been excellently restored. They lead to another of this small park's architectural jewels, the Round House, also designed by Shepley, Rutan & Coolidge. Meant as a shelter, this stone bandstand-style building is in unexpectedly good condition, though the wooden planking is gone, and the first step down to the

The architectural firm of Shepley, Rutan & Coolidge designed and built the Riverway's two stone bridges and the Round House (above) conforming to Olmsted's view that these elements must be subordinate to the overall park design.

dirt floor is a steep one. If you're tall enough, you can get a panorama of the park from here, and an idea of how effectively Olmsted blocked the railroad from view. Just across from this entrance is Short Street and the Winsor School, an elite private school for girls founded in 1886.

Continue along the river path. The landscape opens here somewhat. On the right is the Longwood station of the MBTA and, beyond it, Longwood Towers, which dates to 1928, one of the ornate apartment structures built along the Riverway. The stone wall opposite the station is a popular practice spot for rock climbers. The church with the square-topped steeple is Christ's Church, built in 1860 and designed by Arthur Gilman, the man who laid out the Back Bay street plan and whose other commissions included the Arlington Street Church.

Looming nearer is the granite Shepley, Rutan & Coolidge–designed Longwood Bridge, an immense span for such a narrow park. The bridge, which replaced a rickety wooden predecessor, was built to overarch not only the river but the bridle path and the railroad tracks, and includes pedestrian stairways at each end. It's one of the largest, and was among the most expensive, bridges in the Emerald Necklace.

With attention to detail, the designers bordered the river with stone on each bank at this spot, since grass was unlikely to grow in the shade beneath the bridge.

By now the phragmites have given way to blue and yellow iris, pepperbush, and flowering dogwood at the edges of the river. Farther along the path and on the left is a level gauge that tracks the river's depth and shows just how much the water level varies. On the right, is a Brookline Public Works Department truck yard. The park continues on the other side of Netherlands Road, where a series of small bridges carries the walking trail, and Brookline Avenue beyond, across the river. The Riverway parkway continues from here until it becomes the Jamaicaway and leads to Olmsted Park and Jamaica Pond.

The Riverway is open from 6 a.m. until 11:30 p.m.

The Riverway is bordered by the parkway of the same name, the MBTA Riverside tracks, Park Drive, and Route 9.

How to Get to the Riverway

By subway: The Fenway station of the MBTA Green Line "D" train is at the Landmark Center end of the park, Brookline Village is at the other end, and Longwood is in the middle.

By car: From the West, take Route 128 (I-95) to Route 9 East. Follow Route 9 for about 10 miles. Take a left onto Brookline Avenue. The park is on your left. Or take the Massachusetts Turnpike (I-90) to the Prudential Center exit. At the end of the exit, go straight on

Joggers find the well-maintained path-ways throughout the Emerald Necklace a welcome alternative to city streets.

Huntington Avenue. Take a right onto Longwood Avenue. Longwood runs directly to the park.

From the North or South, take I-93 to the Storrow Drive exit. Follow Storrow Drive to the Kenmore Square exit; access to the exit will be on the left. Take a right onto Beacon Street through Kenmore Square to St. Mary's Street. Take a left onto St. Mary's. The park is on your right.

From Cambridge, take Massa-chusetts Avenue across the John Harvard Bridge. Take a right when you get to Huntington Avenue and a right onto Longwood Avenue. Longwood runs directly to the park.

Parking: There is no park-ing on the streets immedi-ately adjacent to the Riverway. There is limited metered parking on Brook-line Avenue and at the Longwood MBTA stop, off-street parking at Landmark Center, and several parking garages at the hospitals adja-cent to the park.

Olmsted Park

One of Boston's best-kept secrets, Olmsted Park is as true to its original natural condition as the Riverway is

Ward's Pond, one of three man-made bodies of water found in Olmsted Park, offers visitors quiet contemplation of the local flora.

artificial. Its thick mass of old-growth woods hides deep kettle ponds, a small brook, a glacial drum-lin, and other ancient features. All are so effectively screened from the adjacent Jamaicaway that even many Bostonians have no idea there is anything more than a strip of trees along the road to Franklin Park.

Built at about the same time as the Riverway and opened in 1891, this park, too, straddles the Boston-Brookline boundary. Originally divided into two parks, one called Leverett Park and the other called

Jamaica Park, it was merged and renamed for Frederick Law Olmsted after he retired in 1895.

Olmsted Park still has two distinct divisions. One is centered around the nine-acre Leverett Park Woods; the other circles 10-acre Nickerson Hill. Leverett Park Woods is a forest comprised primarily of aged hardwoods. A bridle path parallel to Riverdale Parkway on the Brookline side was converted to a bicycle trail in 1989. Nickerson Hill is a glacial drumlin, surrounded by some of the most natural forest in the Emerald Necklace and adjacent to one of those secluded kettle holes, Ward's Pond.

Of Man and Nature
The park is not entirely untamed. Leverett Pond itself, for instance, was man-made, excavated from the marshy south end of the Muddy River. It was originally intended to become a zoological garden with live animals and birds, but supporters of the idea failed to raise enough money. Nor does this park remain entirely faithful to the design of the man whose name it bears. Olmsted's rolling meadow was leveled and converted to a ball field, for example, and mountain laurel and rhododendron were planted around Ward's Pond by well-meaning devotees.

But where the park has been changed, it is mostly by the elements. Underbrush has overgrown some of the original trails, whose paths are evident now only from the stumps of ruined lampposts. New trees have sprouted from the fallen trunks of old ones.

A Walking Tour of Olmsted Park

Olmsted Park lies between Riverdale Avenue in Brookline and the Jamaicaway in Boston, extending south of the Riverway park to Jamaica Pond. It consists of about 180 acres, including meadows, woodlands, ponds, and streams, along predominantly natural glacial terrain.

From the parking lot on Willow Pond Road, walk north past the Daisy Field ball field and along the Jamaicaway (which should be on your right). Northern red oaks line both side of the Jamaicaway, and uncut blocks of granite separate it from the park. These gradually give way to a barrier of trees between the pathway and the road—the Leverett Park Woods.

The trail here is lined with ancient oaks, elms, and maples; lilacs shoot up from the groundcover. About 100 yards from the parking area, sliver-barked white oaks tower above the thicket. But while in other parks the trees are largely ornamental and meant to be considered on their own, in this park the intended effect is of a thick collected mass of trees and understory. Olmsted meant these woods to be the scenic backdrop for Leverett Pond, now coming into sight below, when viewed from the opposite side in Brookline.

Gulls converge on a tiny island in the pond, and shorebirds totter at the edges. As the trail rounds the pond, the trees thin out, giving way to a jarring view of a high concrete apartment building and a busy road

Leverett Pond was originally intended to become a zoological garden filled with animals and birds. While the plan was never realized, seagulls frequently gather on a tiny island in the pond. The newly created bicycle trail just beyond was originally a bridle path.

Tranquillity abounds in Olmsted Park where dense forest growth masks nearby city intrusions.

beyond. The pathway recoils and joins the bridle-path-turned-bicycle-trail on the Brookline edge of Leverett Pond. From there, Olmsted's scheme to use the facing forest as a backdrop is apparent. But so is an unfortunate 20th-century addition: a hulking Veterans Administration hospital that all but spoils the picture.

On the other hand, there's far less traffic, noise, or litter on this side. Songbirds are able to make themselves heard, ducks paddle by, weeping willows trail in the water, and there is even the white flash of the occasional birch tree. Across Willow Pond Road, which also empties onto this side of the park, is tiny Willow Pond, overhung with willows and fringed with marsh grasses in an archetypal Olmsted landscape.

Tiny stone bridges beckon inward into the Nickerson Woods, as the terrain ascends. Here there are haphazard trails under a cool covering of branches. Smaller vegetation has grown up in the ancient trunks and roots of fallen trees. There was once an organized network of trails here, but these pathways have long since developed minds (and new routes) of their own. Distinctive in the crowd are silver maples more than 120 feet tall and smooth-barked elms.

The trail swings back toward Riverdale Parkway. Just ahead along the road on the right are two municipal athletic fields, Robinson Playground and Harry Downs Field. At this point, take the trail on the left back into the woods to Ward's Pond.

This pond truly looks like a painting. Lily pads float on its surface, and it is ringed with thick trees, mountain laurel, and rhododendron. There is a path around it, and two sets of stone steps designed to look like something from a ruin. One leads to the peak of the Nickerson Woods drumlin, the other back out of Olmsted Park and toward Jamaica Pond.

Olmsted Park is open from 6 a.m. until 11:30 p.m.

Olmsted Park is bordered by the Jamaicaway in Boston, Riverdale Parkway in Brookline, Route 9 and Jamaica Pond.

How to Get to Olmsted Park

By subway: Take the MBTA Green Line "E" train or Bus 39 to the corner of Huntington Avenue and Heath Street. Walk along Huntington (which becomes Boylston Street under the Jamaicaway bridge) in the same direction as the outbound trolley for one block. The park is on the left. Or take the Green Line "D" train to Brookline Village. Follow the path to Route 9. The park is directly across Route 9.

By car: From the West, take Route 128 (I-95) to Route 9 East. Follow Route 9 to the Jamaicaway exit. Follow the Jamaicaway to Willow Pond Road.

From the North or South, take I-93 to the Storrow Drive exit. Follow Storrow Drive to the Kenmore Square exit; access to the exit will be on the left. Take a right onto Beacon Street through Kenmore Square to St. Mary's Street. Take a left onto St. Mary's and a right onto the Riverway. Shortly after the Riverway becomes the Jamaicaway, take a right onto Willow Pond Road.

From Cambridge, take Massachusetts Avenue across the John Harvard Bridge. Take a right on Huntington Avenue and a right onto Longwood Avenue. Take a left from Longwood onto the Riverway. Shortly after the Riverway becomes

the Jamaicaway, take a right onto Willow Pond Road.

Parking: There is free parking at the corner of the Jamaicaway and Willow Pond Road. The entrance is on Willow Pond Road.

Jamaica Pond

Where other Boston parks were built in place of smelly, polluted swamps, Jamaica Pond was considered so pristine it furnished the city's freshwater and ice, and was the center of a colony of summer homes for the elite. There was little debate when Frederick Law Olmsted proposed that it become a link in the Emerald Necklace, and few alterations were required. The beauty of a park, said Olmsted, "should be the beauty of the fields, the meadow, the prairie, and the still waters." About the only major work at Jamaica Pond was in dismantling and removing the ice-houses and all but one of the summer homes that surrounded it by 1890, when the park was approved.

Originally a section of the independent town of Roxbury, Jamaica Plain reputedly was named for the Jamaican rum trade that contributed significantly to this area's economy. But it was water, not rum,

for which Jamaica Pond was prized. By the late 18th century, Boston residents relied for freshwater on rain barrels, local wells, and William Blackstone's spring on Boston Common. Not surprisingly, these were becoming inadequate. Private suppliers eyed Jamaica Pond as a new source, and it became America's first public water reservoir. After all, at 65.5 acres, it was (and, of course, remains) the city's largest naturally occurring body of freshwater. The water was delivered through a network of wooden pipes made from tree trunks until the mid-19th century, when the steadily increasing population overtaxed it and the pond was replaced by Lake Cochituate as Boston's water source in 1848.

Another generation of entrepreneurs began to use the pond around that time as a source of pure freshwater for brewing beer, attracting a colony of German brewers and explaining why so many of the streets in Jamaica Plain have German names. At their peak, there were 22 breweries in Jamaica Plain, more breweries per capita than in any other U.S. city. In the winter, the water was harvested as ice, increasingly valuable for preserving fish and other goods in shipment—and increasingly faddish among the wealthy to keep their drinks cold. Those same upper classes started buying up the farms that ringed the pond and building summer estates there. At the time, Jamaica Plain was still distant enough from downtown Boston to be considered "the country."

That is precisely what attracted Olmsted and the Boston Parks Commission, which purchased 122 acres—including the entire pond. They removed the icehouses and dismantled all the summer homes except one, the Pinebank mansion, which remains. The park was opened in 1892. The existing vegetation was largely left alone, the banks of the pond were shored up slightly and a walking trail added. In 1910 a boathouse and gazebo were constructed just off the Jamaicaway.

A Park Teeming With Life

Jamaica Pond is one of the city's most popular parks, contributing to the resurgence of the neighborhoods off nearby Centre Street, where there are trendy restaurants and shops. The 1.49-mile walking path is a constant blur of runners and walkers. Boats and small sailboats are rented out between May and November, and there is a narrow sand beach. Bufflehead, goldeneye, merganser, wood, and ruddy ducks make their homes here—some year-round—along with mallards, Canada geese, orioles, grackles, cormorants, and swans. The pond is also stocked with trout and pickerel, bass, hornpout, salmon, and perch. Each October, thousands turn out for the annual Lantern Light Parade, circling the pond at dusk with home-made or store-bought lanterns. Children come in costume. In the winter, the hills along the east side of the park are a favorite for sledding.

A Walking Tour of Jamaica Pond

A kettle pond left 15,000 years ago by a retreating glacier, Jamaica Pond is deceptively deep—more than 50 feet in some places. Signs of the glacier can be seen around it in striations on exposed rock. The park extends from Perkins Street and Parkman Drive on the west to the Jamaicaway.

Begin at the corner of Perkins Street and the Jamaicaway, where

The Jamaica Pond boathouse was added in 1910. Rowboats and canoes were once in service, selected as much to enhance the idyllic scene as for their recreational value.

the pond connects with the rest of Olmsted Park across Max Warburg Square. This square is named for a young Boston boy who died of leukemia in 1991 and whose courage in the face of the disease inspired a new curriculum in local schools. One set of steps from Ward's Pond leads here. On the Jamaica Pond side of the street begins a gently sloping meadow that's a favorite sledding area, though one patch has been leveled for a baseball diamond.

The meadow leads down to the tranquil vista of the pond. Follow the path toward the boathouse. Weeping willows droop along the bank, and the trees on the water side of the trail are as evenly spaced as lampposts. As much as they look as if they were planted by man, they are actually river birch that have grown wildly here, though parks workers have cut "windows" in the line of trees to prevent them from obstructing the water views.

The Jamaica Pond Boathouse

The boathouse and gazebo were designed in 1910 by Edmund Wheelwright, the city architect at the time, whose other works include the Longfellow Bridge, New England Conservatory, Massachusetts Historical Society, Museum of Transportation and Harvard Lampoon building. Most are vastly different from one another, not the least of them the buildings at Jamaica Pond, which have been variously described as German Gothic and Tudor Revival. They were restored in 1991. The Boston Park Rangers have a nature center on the first floor of the gazebo; the upper level is open for more sedentary users of the park to sit and look out at the view. Generations of

Small boats and sailboats are available for rental on Jamaica Pond, originally a kettle hole formed by an ancient glacier.

What Have I Caught?

Once a kettle hole formed by an ancient glacier, Jamaica Pond plunges to more than 50 feet in depth. Natural springs make it the largest and purest body of water in Boston.

The state of Massachusetts stocks the pond, and anglers young and old come here to catch trout and the indigenous fish: trout, pickerel, bass, hornpout, and perch.

A fishing license is required. It can be obtained at the Boston Parks Commission at 33 Beacon Street or online (with a credit card) at:
www.sport.state.ma.us/

Brook Trout
Salvelinus fontinalis
8 to 16 inches

sweethearts have carved their names into the thick wooden timbers. A flag on a ship's mast flies above the elaborate entrance gate flanked by the boathouse and gazebo, beyond which boats can be rented.

Before continuing along the loop, notice the woods that frame the scene as viewed from here. On the banks just to the right is a boundary forest, preserved by Olmsted largely from the existing trees, to serve as a backdrop for the pond. This is also a good vantage point to see the single tiny willow-covered island.

Follow the path with the water on your right, curving past the miniscule strip of sandy beach. Here, on Parkman Drive, begins a narrow 8.5-acre forest on a shallow slope. The sugar and silver maples, oak, beech, white pine, and sycamore trees get thicker as the path continues, forming a cover of branches. The trail itself was built with gravel and loam and braced by granite when the banks were shored up by Olmsted.

The Parkman Memorial

Across the road where Parkman Drive meets Perkins Street is the Allerton Overlook, dominated by a Daniel Chester French memorial to Francis Parkman, who had a summer home nearby. Parkman, who died at 70 in 1893, was one of the earliest American historians to chronicle the European settlement of North America. French depicts a chieftain in Iroquois dress representing the five Indian nations about which Parkman was the first to write in a scholarly fashion. The granite monument, which stands 20 feet high, was installed in 1906, and is framed by thick hemlock, cucumber, tulip, magnolia, and walnut trees.

Pinebank

The trail curves around past Pinebank, the last remaining house within the park. The most historic element of this mansion is the steps. They were taken from the patio of John Hancock's house on Beacon Hill, just before it was torn down to make way for an expansion of the State House. The rest of Pinebank is in disrepair and is off-limits, though it is slated for renovation. On this slope of the park is another 8.5-acre boundary forest of huge shade trees, including scatterings of oaks and copper beeches planted here by Olmsted.

The walking trail curves around again and parallels the Jamaicaway, where there remain some handsome mansions and a few more recent, ill-advised additions. The house at 350 the Jamaicaway, unique for its shamrock decorations, was owned by James Michael Curley, the most colorful politician in a city of colorful

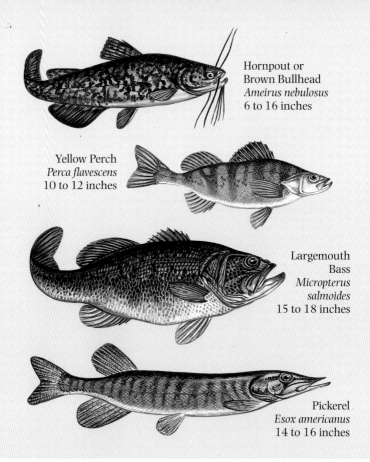

Hornpout or
Brown Bullhead
Ameirus nebulosus
6 to 16 inches

Yellow Perch
Perca flavescens
10 to 12 inches

Largemouth
Bass
*Micropterus
salmoides*
15 to 18 inches

Pickerel
Esox americanus
14 to 16 inches

politicians. A son of Irish immigrants, Curley became a state representative, governor, and congressman. But he is generally remembered as mayor, a position he held intermittently from 1914 until 1950. Even while indicted for setting up a phony mining syndicate, "the Rascal King" won back his seat in City Hall in 1945 by the largest margin ever up to that time. Convicted and imprisoned in 1947, he served only five months before his sentence was commuted by President Harry Truman, and he returned to finish his last term. His house is owned by the city and is used for public functions.

Jamaica Pond is open daily from 6 a.m. until 11:30 p.m. Boats can be rented from noon to dusk between May and November.

Telephone: 617-522-6258.

How to Get to Jamaica Pond
By subway: Take the MBTA Green Line "E" train to the end of the line at Heath Street (Veterans Administration Medical Center). Walk down Craftston Way to the Jamaicaway and take a left. Jamaica Pond will be just under one mile away on your right. Or take Bus 39 from Copley Square or Forest Hills to the intersection of Pond and Centre streets. Walk one block down Pond Street to the park.

By car: From the West, take Route 128 (I-95) to Route 9 East. Follow Route 9 to the Jamaicaway exit. Turn onto the Jamaicaway and follow it to where Jamaica Pond is on your right.

From the North or South, take I-93 to the Storrow Drive exit. Follow Storrow Drive to the Kenmore Square exit; access to the exit will be on the left. Take a right onto Beacon Street through Kenmore Square to St. Mary's Street. Take a left onto St. Mary's and a right onto the Riverway. The Riverway becomes the Jamaicaway. Continue on the Jamaicaway. Jamaica Pond will be on your right.

From Cambridge, take Massachusetts Avenue across the John Harvard Bridge. Take a right on Huntington Avenue and a right onto Longwood Avenue. Take a left from Longwood onto the Riverway. The Riverway becomes the Jamaicaway. Continue on the Jamaicaway. Jamaica Pond will be on your right.

Parking: There is limited nonresident parking on Pond Street, perpendicular to the Jamaicaway and opposite the Jamaica Pond boathouse, and free parking at the corner of the Jamaicaway and Willow Pond Road in Olmsted Park. The parking entrance is on Willow Pond Road.

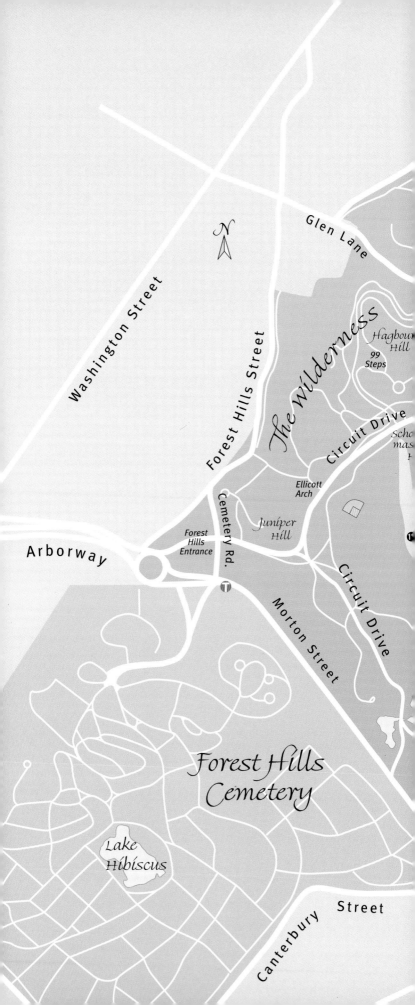

White
Schoolboy
Stadium

Long Crouch Woods

Playstead Road

ite of the
verlook

The Playstead

Pierpont Road

Seaver Street

Old Trail Rd.

P

Glen Lane

Circuit Drive

Franklin
Park Zoo

C 🚻 🚻

Franklin
Park

2

3

1

5

P

11

13

Franklin Park

14

6

Golf Course

4

🚻
C

P

Clubhouse

18

15

Scarboro
Hill

10

9

16   17

Scarboro Pond

7

8

Circuit Drive

Blue Hill Avenue

T

American Legion Highway

Franklin Park

Along with Central Park in Manhattan and Prospect Park in Brooklyn, Boston's Franklin Park is considered one of Frederick Law Olmsted's three greatest works—his greatest, in the opinion of his stepson and successor, John C. Olmsted. The effective end of the Emerald Necklace, Franklin Park was to be separated from the Boston Common by more than just the 6.37-mile walking distance. As the 19th century came to a close, an era when "country parks" were in vogue, this was to be a quiet, rural, passive space where sheep would graze and city residents on walks or carriage rides could be reminded of what life was like in simpler places and times.

Assembling and constructing this serene environment would prove an exercise in aggravation. The site, over 500 acres, had been under consideration for a park since 1876, but the nationwide depression of the 1870s created a shortage of money to buy it. The economy was even worse in Boston, where the great fire of November 1872 had wiped out much of the financial district. The city also had been pressed into taking out a large loan to upgrade its chronically decrepit sewage system. Political infighting between the establishment Brahmins and the newly emergent Irish made things worse. Finally someone in the gov-

ernment remembered that Benjamin Franklin, who was born in Boston, had left the city a bequest that had been earning interest for 100 years. A proposal was made to use it for the park, whose name was promptly changed from West Roxbury Park to Franklin Park in gratitude for the anticipated windfall.

The name change proved premature, however. The city overrode its debt limit to borrow $2.5 million for the project, and Franklin's money wasn't needed. (In the end, the land prices also turned out to be deflated by the economic problems, and the park cost only $600,000 to buy, compared to $4 million for Prospect Park in Brooklyn, which is about the same size). But it was not the end of the financial problems.

Grand Plans

Two thirds of the park was to comprise nothing but rural scenery, with a meadow in the middle grazed by sheep, all surrounded by a stone wall. This was called the Country Park, inspired by Birkenhead Park near Liverpool, England, which Olmsted had visited. He decreed that under no circumstances were large meetings to be held there, or activities allowed—not even scientific study of the trees, as in the Arnold Arboretum. Only naturally occurring trees and flowers would be tolerated, not the exotic species popular

in other parks. This would be a place for relaxation and reflection. The other third would be dominated by the Greeting, a half-mile promenade similar to the Mall in Central Park. There would be a 30-acre field for children called the Playstead, a 100-acre wilderness, a music amphitheater, a deer park, a playground called the Little Folks' Fair, even a tiny dairy. A huge, low-slung shelter was built overlooking the Playstead, with food concessions and locker rooms.

Not much of this went right. Because of economic limitations, the Greeting, the amphitheater, and the Little Folks' Fair were never built. The Boston Historical Society wanted a chunk of the park for a zoo. Political and social groups pushed to hold large gatherings. The play area was overcrowded with enthusiasts playing croquet, archery, and lawn tennis; athletic associations demanded more space. The wall around the Country Park was never finished. The shelter burned down and was not rebuilt. Worse still, attendance at the Country Park was dismal. It turned out people wanted something to do in their parks besides stare passively at trees and rocks. To boost attendance, the sheep meadow was converted to a golf course, the Greeting became a zoo, and a stadium and parade ground were built at the Playstead. Later, another piece of the park was taken away to build a hospital. About 120 acres had been carved away from Olmsted's park.

And Some Come True

There were some successes. Largely at Olmsted's urging, a 100-acre field was purchased nearby for athletic facilities. A man-made water body, Scarboro Pond, was added by the Olmsted firm, to great acclaim. The stadium became the frequent site of national cross-country championships, using pathways through the park as running routes. The golf course, only the second of its kind to open in America, was a huge success. The zoo, after some neglect, has been revitalized. And Franklin Park, straddling as it does three distinctly different sections of the city, has become an interracial meeting place.

A Walking Tour of Franklin Park

Franklin Park accounts for more than half the land area of the entire Emerald Necklace. Built between 1885 and 1898, it lies just east of Jamaica Pond and the Arnold Arboretum. It is possible to drive through parts of this park on Circuit Drive and on Morton Street, which runs between Franklin Park and Forest Hills Cemetery. There are six miles of roads and 15 miles of hiking paths.

While Olmsted envisioned a grand entrance off the Arborway, today

A landscape from the English countryside, with grazing sheep and rural scenery, was Olmsted's original plan for the area named the Country Park. But sparse attendance and the public's preference for more activities eventually led to its conversion to a public golf course.

Glacial Evidence in Boston's Parks

Boston has been so changed by the hand of man that its various parks offer some of the best—and, for that matter, last remaining—places to observe the area's superlative original geology. That story begins nearly half a billion years ago, when North America and Africa collided and created, among other things, the Appalachian Range that separates New England from the rest of the continent. Then, in the comparatively recent period of the last two and a half million years, glaciers advanced to cover all of New England.

The impact of the glaciers, which receded a mere 10,000 years ago, is evident everywhere in Boston's parks. The incremental friction of their movement carved out long narrow ridges called eskers, piled stones and boulders into moraines, blunted the tops of hills, and sculpted oval-shaped mounds called drumlins out of clay and gravel dumped in their wakes. Trapped concentrations of ice left kettle holes such as Jamaica Pond, which filled with water when the glaciers melted. Glaciers also drained to form the Charles, Mystic, and Neponset rivers.

Some of the most prominent, if least evident, drumlins are the Boston Harbor Islands. When the glaciers melted and the ocean levels rose, these drumlins were cut off, making this the only drumlin field in America that intersects the coastline. There are more than 200 drumlins in the Boston Basin, roughly 30 of them in the harbor; some of the islands consist of more than one of the gently shaped mounds. Wind and wave erosion also have helped to mold—and continue to shape—these islands. Human intervention is apparent here, too. Spectacle Island, for example, has been enlarged with fill from the Central Artery construction project, colloquially known as the Big Dig. Some of the islands also feature sandy beaches, and two—Lovells and Long islands—have sand dunes.

The harbor itself is composed of so-called Cambridge argillite, a shalelike rock that dates back about 570 million years. This bedrock is exposed—and can be seen up close—on Great Brewster and Little Brewster islands.

No geologic substance is more prevalent in Boston's parks than the colorfully named Roxbury puddingstone, which was designated Massachusetts' "state rock" in 1983. Puddingstone is a conglomeration of materials gathered by the glaciers,

the first thing visitors who arrive from that direction see is Lemuel Shattuck Hospital. Take the hospital road, staying to the left of the fork, however, and it will quickly lead you to Scarboro Pond, a man-made water body named for John Scarboro, one of the earliest English residents of Roxbury. His farmhouse stood where there are now two tennis courts along the left side of the road. This was originally meant to be the site of the dairy and sheep farm, but Olmsted's sons later redesigned it as a

A boulder of Roxbury puddingstone in Franklin Park. It became a popular building material in the 19th century and was used throughout the Emerald Necklace.

washed by the ocean, and buried under rocks whose weight cemented them together. It was a particularly popular building material in and around Boston in the 19th century, when most of the city's parks were built, and designers including Frederick Law Olmsted used it everywhere. There are puddingstone steps, puddingstone shelters, puddingstone walls, and puddingstone bridges in many of the parks, where puddingstone also occurs naturally in abundance. The greatest amount of it is evident in Franklin Park.

So closely associated with Boston is this type of rock that a 30-ton chunk of it was shipped to Gettysburg in 1886 as a memorial to soldiers of the 20th Massachusetts Regiment who died in the Battle of Gettysburg. The monument was the idea of some surviving veterans who remembered climbing on large puddingstone boulders in Roxbury when they were boys.

scenic vantage point. The pond is surrounded by tupelo, red maple, and dogwood trees.

Just beyond the pond is Scarboro Hill, a glacial drumlin where a stand of European beech and flowering dogwood trees frames a view of Olmsted's meadow, now the golf course, fringed by 33 acres of woods. While Olmsted might not recognize it, this is still one of the most stunning landscapes in the Emerald Necklace.

Double back to the Forest Hills entrance. The path here leads to Juniper Hill, one of the few places in the park laid out as Olmsted first conceived it, with thick copses of red cedars leading down a slope into a valley where there is a shallow brook. Olmsted called this place the Resting Ground. Turn left and go under the Ellicott Arch to see Olmsted's half-mile sheep meadow from another angle. The arch, which is made of boulders, was designed by Olmsted's stepson, John C. Olmsted. It leads to the Wilderness, an 80-acre thickly wooded forest—largest in the Emerald Necklace—crossed by narrow paths and meant to look the way New England did when

When lawn tennis became all the rage in the 1890s, parks workers laid out numerous courts in Franklin Park.

white settlers first arrived in the early 17th century.

One trail cuts across the Wilderness, while a second skirts the edge and enters the forest at its most level point. This was once a bridle path. There are little dells among the oak, hemlock, hickory, walnut, and other hardwoods, and a dark green ground-cover called vinca carpets the forest floor with oval-shaped leaves, punctuated by sudden natural outcroppings of Roxbury puddingstone.

Roaming the Wilderness

Make for the highest point along the bridle path, which meanders toward the park's interior. You'll see one of the foremost surviving architectural elements of Franklin Park: the 99 Steps that lead from Circuit Drive up Hagbourne Hill. The broad slag steps are made of Roxbury puddingstone. Look for another summit just across the road, southeast of here. This is Schoolmaster Hill, named in honor of Ralph Waldo Emerson, who once served as a Roxbury schoolmaster. The view from the top is worthy of a poet. Because of the topography, no signs of human life are evident in the five-mile view that stretches west to Great Blue Hill in Milton.

The trails widen, wind around,

Ellicott Arch, designed in the late 1880s by John Olmsted, is pictured here shortly after its construction. Later photographs show the arch hidden by a an array of small shrubs, vines, and ground-cover plants stuck into the crevices of the boulders.

Manicured greens are a far cry from the conditions players encountered when Franklin Park's golfing days began in December of 1890. Left, bucolic Scarboro Pond, a man-made body of water named for one of Roxbury's earliest English residents.

and converge near the Playstead. On the near side is the Overlook, site of the only building ever designed by Frederick Law Olmsted. The Overlook Shelter was a low-slung wooden building 800 feet long on a foundation of boulders excavated when the field was graded. Meant to be at one with its surroundings, the shelter was planted with vines and shrubs. City architect Arthur Vinal, who also designed the Metropolitan Waterworks in Chestnut Hill and the Orpheum Theatre, contributed a few structural touches and details, including the idea of incorporating two stone columns to support the roof. There was a food concession area upstairs, and locker rooms downstairs through a separate entrance off the Playstead.

Unfortunately, the building burned down in 1945, though the foundation remains. Today it watches over not a green field, but White Schoolboy Stadium, which has been the site of the U.S. cross-country championships in 1917, 1950, 1984, 1991, 1992, and the world championships in 1992. The racing routes are laid out on the walking paths around the wilderness, another far cry from the passive recreation urged by Olmsted.

On the opposite side of the stadium from the Overlook is Long Crouch Woods, a 17-acre forest that was originally meant to screen the Playstead from close-in Seaver Street. Paths were cut through here in 1904, and once there were

fenced-off bear dens in the woods, an attraction dreamed up to increase interest in the zoo. They were removed in 1957.

Walk toward the vehicle exit from the stadium. Directly ahead is one of the two entrances to the Franklin Park Zoo, designed by Olmsted disciple Arthur Shurcliff and opened in 1913. This was meant to be the site of Olmsted's Greeting, the enormous half-mile carriage-riding promenade. At this end are two art deco statues by Daniel Chester French, one each representing Commerce and Industry, which were salvaged from the post office building in Post Office Square when it was torn down and replaced in 1930.

The Golf Course

Take a right. This road leads back toward the golf course. Just before it links back up with Circuit Drive, it's flanked by a pair of original stone shelters. Here riders would wait for public carriages to take them through the Country Park on scenic drives. The carriage shelters were designed by the firm of Shepley, Rutan & Coolidge, which also designed the two bridges over Scarboro Pond, the Forest Hills entrance arch, and the Round House and the bridges in the Riverway, not to mention the Art Institute of Chicago and other notable commissions.

Straight ahead is Franklin Park's 116-acre William J. Devine Golf

Course—also called the Country Meadow Golf Course—second-oldest in the nation. (The oldest is in Van Cortland Park in New York City.) People were golfing in Franklin Park almost as soon as it was opened, which gave the park commissioners the notion that a formal golf course would increase attendance. The earliest recorded round of golf in New England was at Franklin Park in December of 1890. Tomato cans were used for cups. The original nine-hole layout was designed beginning in 1915 by Willie Campbell, the golf pro at The Country Club, a prestigious private course in Brookline. It was so popular it was expanded to 18 holes, and became a melting pot of Jewish, Irish Catholic, and black golfers—a role the public course continues today with an annual tournament called Black and White on Green.

Franklin Park is open daily from dawn to dusk. The Franklin Park Golf Course is open year-round.

The park is bounded by Forest Hills Street, Seaver Street, Blue Hill Avenue, American Legion Highway, and Forest Hills Cemetery. Golf course telephone: 617-265-4084.

How to Get to Franklin Park

By subway: Take the MBTA Orange Line to Forest Hills station, then walk three blocks to the park.

By car: from Boston or Cambridge, take Storrow Drive to the Fenway exit. Follow the Fenway to the Riverway, the Jamaicaway, then the Arborway (Route 203 East), bearing left onto the overpass. The entrance to the park is at the end of the overpass, around the rotary.

From the west, take the Massachusetts Turnpike (I-90) to the Allston exit. Follow the signs to Storrow Drive. Follow Storrow Drive inbound (toward downtown Boston) to the Fenway exit. Follow the Fenway to the Riverway, which becomes the Jamaicaway and then the Arborway. After passing the Arnold Arboretum, bear left to go over the overpass. The entrance to the park is at the end of the overpass, around the rotary.

From the south, take Exit 15 from the Southeast Expressway. At the end of the exit, take a left onto Columbia Road, being careful to follow Columbia Road where it takes a left at the third traffic signal. From there, continue on Columbia Road through nine more traffic signals. After crossing Blue Hill Avenue, look for the park on the left.

Parking: There is plenty of free parking near the entrance to the zoo, at the golf course clubhouse, outside White Stadium, and along most park roads.

Of the forest antelopes, the bongo is the largest and most colorful. What the bongo lacks in speed it makes up for in its keen sense of hearing and its ability to jump great heights. Found mainly in the forests of eastern, central, and western Africa, bongos travel solo, in pairs, or in small groups of females with their young and one male. Males can weigh as much as 600 pounds, females up to 540 pounds; newborns weigh in at an impressive 48-plus pounds.

*Franklin Farm
features a "contact
corral," where
children can pet
goats and sheep.
The main barn
houses a cow,
ponies, and
miniature horses.
Visitors may also
view newly hatched
chicks in the incu-
bator and brooder
building.*

Franklin Park Zoo

Nostalgic for the farms where he apprenticed as a young man in Connecticut, Frederic Law Olmsted was determined to expose the increasingly cosmopolitan people of Boston to the agrarian lifestyle they were already beginning to forget. He called for a dairy, a sheep pasture, and a deer park to be included inside Franklin Park, in a section he distinguished as the Meadow, part of an enormous area Olmsted dubbed the Country Park. He also planned a children's area he named Playstead. But as with many of Olmsted's plans in Franklin Park, competing interests foiled these ideas. An athletic stadium was ultimately built in place of the fields at Playstead, and the sheep meadow was turned into an 18-hole golf course. In all, about 120 acres of the original park area have been whittled away for other uses. And when the dairy and deer park failed to attract much interest, the city bowed to pressure from the Boston Natural Historical Society and handed over nearly 80 acres for a zoo.

Construction began in 1911. In 1913, the first building, the birdhouse, designed by William Austin, opened. Its proponents had ambitious plans for their zoo, though they generally had to make do with architectural cast offs. When a tower was added to the Greek Revival–style Custom House building downtown in 1916, for example, eight granite Doric columns removed from the original Custom House atrium were reassembled here to provide a formal entrance, named Peabody Circle after architect and parks commis-

Few animals match the rare beauty and quiet mystery of the snow leopard. Elusive and solitary, they live in remote pockets of central Asia. People seldom see these animals in the wild; however a successful breeding program has been going on in zoos for years.

The oldest building in the zoo, Bird's World opened in 1913. The building, built with a Far Eastern motif in mind, houses a variety of species of birds as well as reptiles.

sioner Robert Peabody. And when the post office building at Post Office Square was removed in 1930, two art deco statues—representing Commerce and Industry—were scavenged for the Pierpont Road approach.

A Zoo in Decline . . .

The zoo was only slightly more successful than the deer park in attracting public enthusiasm. Dressing it up on the outside did little to halt the declining attendance that worsened during the Depression and World War II. Increasingly neglected, the zoo became prone to vandalism. In 1958, the city handed it over to the Metropolitan District Commission, which built a children's section, animal hospital, and administrative offices. Still, interest continued to be low. The decline of the surrounding neighborhood also discouraged visitors. The zoo was twice named one of the worst in the country during the 1980s, and an investigation by the Massachusetts Society for the Prevention of Cruelty to Animals

called it inhumane, saying poor conditions had contributed to the deaths of eight animals.

. . . And in Revival

The opening of the indoor tropical forest in 1989 reignited interest. The largest indoor open-space zoo exhibit in North America, with 150 animals, it attracted nearly 14,000 people in its first weekend and 120,000 in its first four months. Things were starting to look up. In 1991, the private Commonwealth Zoological Corporation (now called Zoo New England) was created to take over management of the Franklin Park Zoo and its sister zoo, the Stone Zoo in Stoneham. Attendance rose to its current 500,000 a year.

Today there are more than 220 species of animals in the 72-acre zoo, many of them representing species that are threatened or endangered. The zoo has a trio of African wild dogs, for instance, the most endangered large carnivores in Africa; fewer than 5,000 are believed to survive in the wild.

Kookaburra—the common name for this squat, long-tailed Australian kingfisher— is also known as the laughing jackass because of its maniacal-sounding call.

Mandarin ducks nest in tree cavities or on the ground, producing up to 12 eggs that hatch in 30 days.

The magnificent peacock is quarrelsome and does not mix well with other domestic animals. Peacocks fly surprisingly well, despite their size, and roost in trees at night. During courtship the crested male common peacock displays his elongated upper tail coverts—a spectacular green and gold erectile train adorned with blue-green "eyes"—before the duller-plumaged female.

Instead of cages, many of the animals are kept in mixed-species exhibits. The four-acre Bongo Congo exhibit, for example, just inside the main entrance, includes ibex, ostriches, and plains zebras. Across the path is the George Robert White Children's Zoo, with exotic species including prairie dogs and snow leopards, and a wooden walkway that crosses a small duck pond.

A Walking Tour of the Franklin Park Zoo

The Franklin Park Zoo runs along the eastern edge of Franklin Park, with entrances at two ends. The Zebra Entrance is near the intersection of Columbia Road and Blue Hill Avenue on the perimeter of the park. The Giraffe Entrance is inside the park, near White Stadium on Pierpont Road. There is ample parking near both entrances, though the closest parking is at the Giraffe Entrance. Most exhibits are along a main pathway that runs between the two gates.

Enter at the Giraffe Entrance. Inside are the towering art deco statues by Daniel Chester

A century ago, African wild dog packs numbering a hundred or more animals could be seen roaming the Serengeti Plains in Southern Africa. Today, the total population on the Serengeti is probably less than 60 dogs.

Wallabies are marsupials— that is, their young develop in a pouch. At birth, the new-born wallaby leaves the birth canal, makes its way to its mothers pouch, and feeds there until it is about 7 months old. Nocturnal and solitary, wallabies congregate only at feeding sites, where they dine on grasses and herbs.

Although Baird's tapir, right, resembles a pig, it is more closely related to the horse and rhinoceros. Its long nose is its most valuable asset. It's sensitive to touch and smell and can pull leaves and shoots into the animal's mouth.

Visitors to Butterfly Landing walk amid 1,000 butterflies in free flight. Approximately 45 different species of North American butterflies are on exhibit.

cackles; golden-breasted starlings from East Africa, which feed on termites, their favorite food; and a Bali mynah bird, rare in the wild but now on the increase in captivity.

The Australian Outback Trail

The path leads from Bird's World directly to the Australian Outback Trail—two trails, actually, where only rope fences separate guests from the wallabies, kangaroos, and emus that make up this mixed species exhibit. The red kangaroos on display can bound nearly 30 feet in a single hop. Wallabies are marsupials like kangaroos and resemble them, though the ones here have distinctive red necks. Emus are flightless birds with small wings and heavy bodies.

Continue along the main walkway. To the left is the Giraffe Savannah, which houses two Masai giraffes added to the zoo in 1999. These giraffes have eight-foot necks, and the highest blood pressure of any warm-blooded animal, which is necessary to pump blood to their heads. There are also endangered Grevys zebras here. To the right is a tented seasonal butterfly enclosure 174 feet long and 21 feet tall called Butterfly Landing, with nearly 45 species of butterflies—1,000 butterflies in all—plus gardens, a waterfall, and soft music. It's open from late May through September. There are also caterpillars and chrysalises, the sacks in which caterpillars turn to butterflies.

Next door is the Franklin Farm

French. Immediately through the entrance to the right is one of the oldest structures in the zoo, William Austin's original birdhouse. The Oriental-style Bird's World is divided today into various habitats, from swamp to desert. It and the adjacent outdoor flight cage house not only birds but reptiles, including turtles, Gila monsters, anacondas, and a Burmese python. Among the birds here are Andean condors, one of the world's largest birds of prey. Their wingspan can reach 12 feet and they weigh as much as 25 pounds. Condors can live up to 100 years in the wild. In captivity their lifespan sometimes exceeds that. There are also fat-billed Australian kookaburra birds, whose calls sound like human

The capybara—the name means "master of the grasses"—is the largest member of the rodent family. Barrel-shaped with short legs, it seems awkward on land but is a good swimmer.

The largest of the African carnivores, these "kings of the jungle" are at home in the African grassland and live in family groups, or prides, of between 3 and 30. Although male lions dominate this society, females like the one pictured are the principle hunters.

The emu is a large flightless bird found only in Australia. It is the second largest bird in the world— only the ostrich is bigger. Emus can run very fast and can also swim. They normally live in large flocks in grass plains and open forests eating grass, insects, fruit, and seeds. They make funny grunting noises and the females also make a booming noise.

Despite its ungainly appearance the ostrich holds the distinction of being the world's largest bird. It runs faster than any other two-legged animal and lays the largest eggs of any living creature. Like humans, the ostrich has long eyelashes, mainly to keep dust from getting in its eyes.

exhibit that would no doubt please Olmsted. It includes tame Nigerian dwarf goats and sheep that young visitors are encouraged to pet, and a big brown cow, and so-called Plymouth Rock chickens, from a breed with striking bright red combs.

In the Children's Zoo there are prairie dogs, porcupines, tortoises, frogs, snakes, and lizards, and a magnificent snow leopard.

Bongo Congo and Kalahari Kingdom

The four-acre Bongo Congo exhibit comes up next on the left. Here are housed more plains zebras; ostriches that can grow up to eight feet high and weigh 265 pounds; rare Nubian ibexes—the males with huge curving horns—which have all but vanished in the wild; and white-bearded wildebeests. Guests can look in from two thatched observation posts on stilts.

Beyond that is Kalahari Kingdom, where visitors get up close and personal with a pair of African lions. Here the zoo's modest size is an advantage, as it's possible to get closer to the lions than at many other zoos. Guests can climb into a "crashed" Land Rover and see the lions through the windshield, or watch them from across a moat or from a "ranger station."

Tropical Forest

From here the trail loops around to the three-acre indoor Tropical Forest. It's not much to look at from the outside, made as it is from long-span steel arches with a translucent fiberglass-reinforced fabric hung from a network of cables, but it remains a favorite on the inside. There are tropical birds, including saddle-billed storks, alongside cotton-top tamarins, a kind of monkey with a white furry mane of wispy hair; pottos, or lemurlike prosimians; baboons, warthogs, mandrills, DeBrazza's monkeys, pygmy hippos, capybaras—all in a naturally lit rain forest with amplified jungle sounds. The gorillas housed here are particularly popular, including a western lowland gorilla born at the zoo in

Weighing in at 600 pounds, adult male western lowland gorillas—called silverbacks— stand 5 to 6 feet tall with powerful arms stretching 7 to 8 feet across. The largest and strongest of all primates, they are also among the least aggressive.

1999. There's a black leopard, an African vulture, and a Baird's tapir—a relative of the horse but with a long pointed nose it can use as a snorkel when hiding underwater. Those African wild dogs live just outside this building. Among the other residents of the Tropical Forest are bats, pythons, dwarf crocodiles, and 17 species of free flight birds.

The Franklin Park Zoo is open daily except Thanksgiving and Christmas. From April 1 through September 30: hours are 10 a.m. to 5 p.m. weekdays and 10 a.m. to 6 p.m. weekends and holidays. From October 1 through March 31: hours are 10 a.m. to 4 p.m. daily. Admission is $7 for adults, $6 for seniors, and $4 for children ages 2 through 15. There is an additional $1 fee to enter the Butterfly Landing.

The zoo is located at 1 Franklin Park Road. Telephone: 617-541-LION.

How to Get to the Zoo

By subway: Take the MBTA Orange Line to Forest Hills station, then take Bus 16 to the zoo. Bus 16 also connects to the zoo from Andrew station on the Red Line.

By car: from Boston or Cambridge, take Storrow Drive to the Fenway exit. Follow the Fenway to the Jamaicaway to the Arborway to Route 203 East and look for the signs to the zoo. From Route 9, take the Jamaicaway to Route 203 East, bearing left to go over the overpass. At the next rotary, follow the signs to the zoo.

From the west, take the Massachusetts Turnpike (I-90) to the Allston exit. Follow the signs to Storrow Drive. Follow Storrow Drive inbound (toward downtown Boston) to the Fenway exit. Follow the Fenway to the Riverway, which becomes the Jamaicaway and then the Arborway. After passing the Arnold Arboretum, bear left to go over the overpass. At the next rotary, follow the signs to the zoo.

From the south, take Exit 15 from the Southeast Expressway. At the end of the exit, take a left onto Columbia Road, being careful to follow Columbia Road where it takes a left at the third traffic signal. From there, continue on Columbia Road through nine more traffic signals. After crossing Blue Hill Avenue, look for the zoo on the left.

Parking: There is plenty of free parking at the zoo entrances.

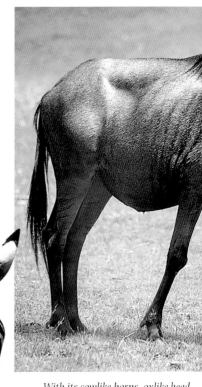

With its cowlike horns, oxlike head, brown bands on its neck and shoulders, and white beard, it's hard to tell that the white-bearded wildebeest, above, is a member of the antelope family.

Although zebras seem conspicuous to us, in fact their stripes provide them great camouflage in the high grass. Like human fingerprints, the striping pattern is unique to each zebra.

The giraffe is the world's tallest animal, measuring up to 18 feet in height. Despite its length and flexibility, the neck is too short to easily reach the ground. In order to drink water or eat grass, the animal must awkwardly spread its legs wide so its head can reach the ground.

Arnold Arboretum

Faulkner Hospital

CENTRE

Centre Street Gate

PLANE TREES

Dana Greenhouses

Bonsai House

DWARF CONIFER

SILVERBELLS

HICKORIES

VALLEY ROAD

SWEETGUMS

WALNUTS

BUSSEY HILL ROAD

BIRCHES

ZELKOVAS

CHERRIES

North Woods

BUSSEY HILL ROAD

ELMS

OAKS

Oak Path

LILACS

AZALEAS

Bussey Hill 198 ft.

CATALPAS

VALLEY ROAD

DOVE TREE

Chinese Path

CEDARS OF LEBANON

FRANKLINIAS

ASHES

LOCUSTS

STEWARTIAS

BEECHES

Beech Path

Beech Path

FORSYTHIAS

FOREST

Linda J. Davison Rhododendron Path

Beech Path Gate

CONIFERS

SOUTH STREET

South Street Gate

SOUTH STREET

SOUTH STREET

Stony Brook Marsh

WASHINGTON

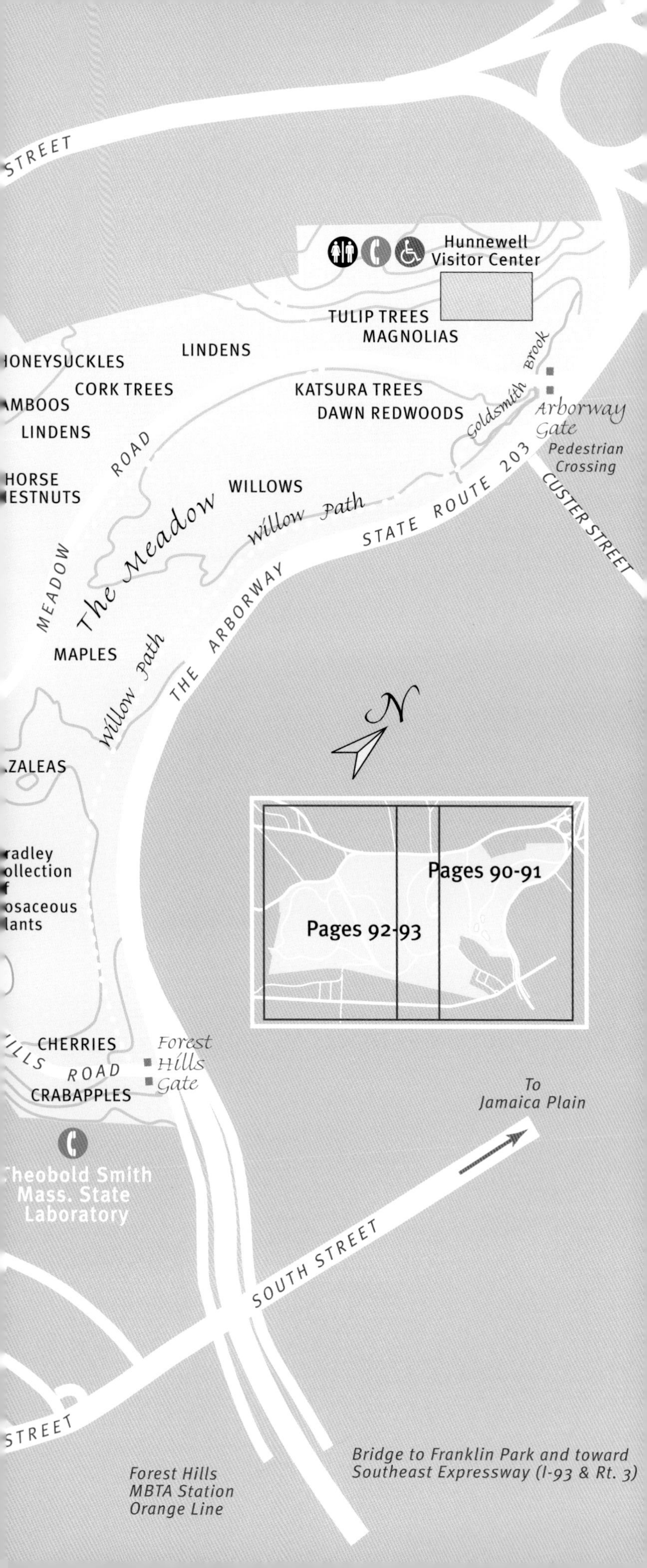

STREET

HONEYSUCKLES

LINDENS

CORK TREES

BAMBOOS

LINDENS

Hunnewell
Visitor Center

TULIP TREES
MAGNOLIAS

KATSURA TREES
DAWN REDWOODS

Goldsmith Brook

Arborway
Gate
Pedestrian
Crossing

HORSE CHESTNUTS

ROAD

The Meadow

WILLOWS

Willow Path

STATE ROUTE 203

CUSTER STREET

MEADOW

Willow Path

THE ARBORWAY

MAPLES

N

AZALEAS

Bradley
Collection
of
Rosaceous
Plants

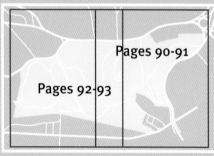

Pages 90-91

Pages 92-93

CHERRIES

HILLS ROAD

Forest
Hills
Gate

CRABAPPLES

To
Jamaica Plain

Theobold Smith
Mass. State
Laboratory

STREET

SOUTH STREET

Forest Hills
MBTA Station
Orange Line

Bridge to Franklin Park and toward
Southeast Expressway (I-93 & Rt. 3)

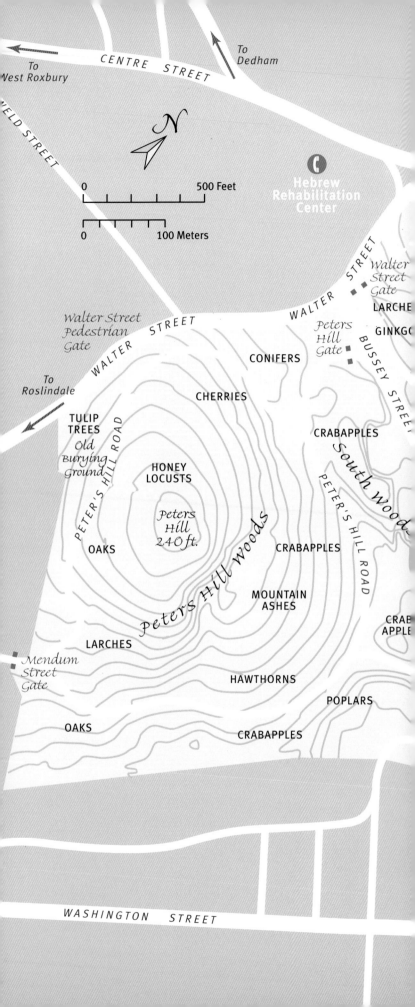

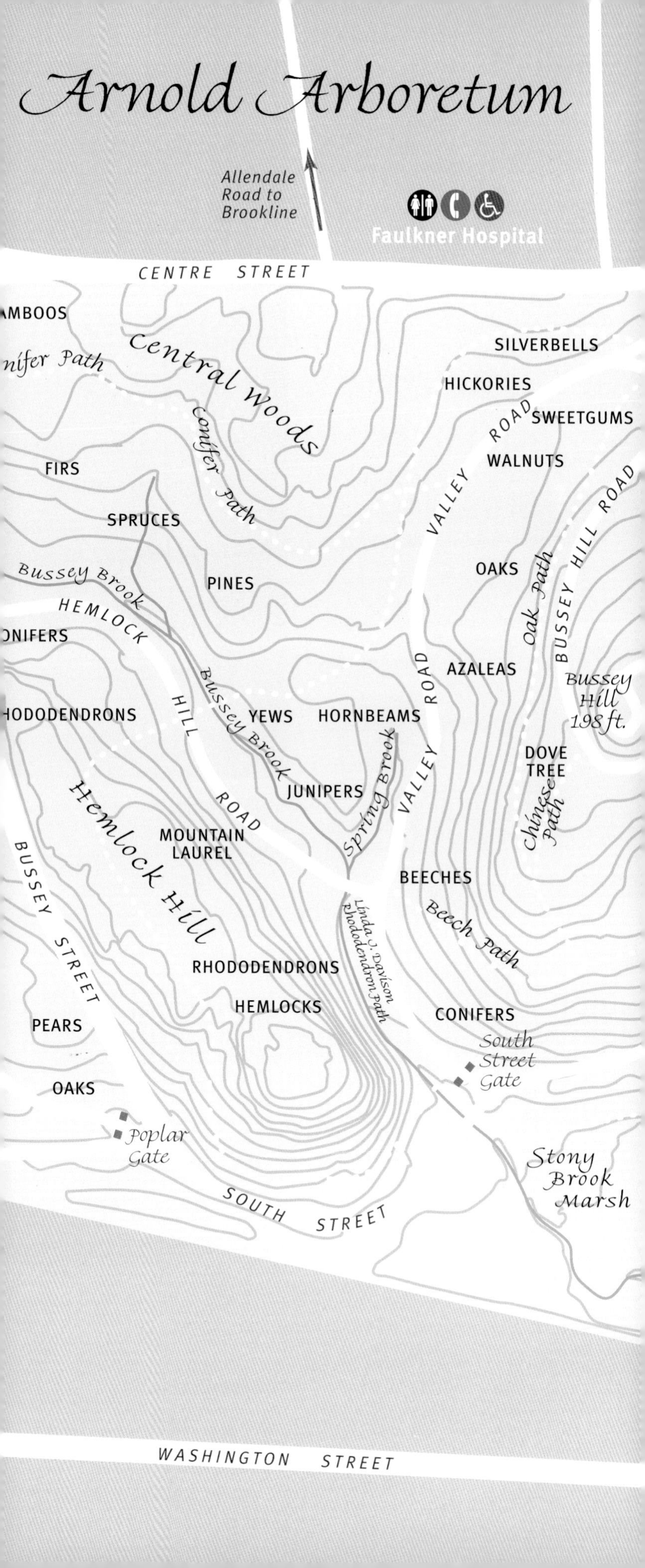

Arnold Arboretum

Allendale
Road to
Brookline

Faulkner Hospital

CENTRE STREET

BAMBOOS

Conifer Path

Central Woods

SILVERBELLS

HICKORIES

SWEETGUMS

VALLEY ROAD

WALNUTS

FIRS

Conifer Path

SPRUCES

OAKS

BUSSEY HILL ROAD

Bussey Brook

PINES

HEMLOCK

CONIFERS

AZALEAS

Oak Path

Bussey
Hill
198 ft.

RHODODENDRONS

HILL

Bussey Brook

YEWS

HORNBEAMS

VALLEY ROAD

DOVE
TREE

JUNIPERS

Spring Brook

Chinese Path

ROAD

MOUNTAIN
LAUREL

Hemlock Hill

BEECHES

Beech Path

Linda J. Davison Rhododendron Path

BUSSEY STREET

RHODODENDRONS

HEMLOCKS

CONIFERS

South
Street
Gate

PEARS

OAKS

Poplar
Gate

Stony
Brook
Marsh

SOUTH STREET

WASHINGTON STREET

The Arnold Arboretum

One of the most renowned botanical gardens in the United States, the Arnold Arboretum is a product of a reluctant partnership between Harvard University and the city of Boston. Neither really wanted to join forces on the arboretum, but the project has immeasurably benefited both.

The Idea of an Arboretum

Natural history was still a science practiced primarily by amateurs—mainly wealthy gentleman farmers who had gardens on their large estates—when the idea of adding an arboretum to Harvard was first raised in the mid-1800s. The impetus was not necessarily the pursuit of knowledge but, as with so many things in Boston, a lack of room. Harvard's small botanical garden in Cambridge, which had opened in 1805, comprised only seven acres; and the director, Asa Gray, was beginning to come around to the idea of adding trees.

There was also growing community interest in the issue. New museums were in fashion, and what was an arboretum but a living museum? Prominent Bostonians including George Barrell Emerson, headmaster of a private girls' school, were pushing for a public tree collection.

There had been talk of putting an arboretum at the Public Garden site in Boston as early as 1841. And in 1870, Henry Wadsworth Longfellow proposed that Harvard build an arboretum on land between his house on Brattle Street and the Charles River. (Not coincidentally, a slaughterhouse had been planned for the site, which would have spoiled Longfellow's unimpeded river view.)

Fortuitous Bequests

Outside events were soon to come to bear on this decision. Harvard had been left a portion of a 394-acre estate in the Jamaica Plain section of West Roxbury by Benjamin Bussey, a businessman and gentleman farmer. Bussey had allowed the public on his wooded property, even providing paths and benches. When he willed it to the university upon his death in 1842, it was with the stipulation that Harvard run an agricultural and horticultural school there—and that his other heirs be allowed to live on the property for as long as they wanted.

Meanwhile, in 1868, James Arnold, a rich New Bedford merchant who was also an amateur gardener, left $103,847.57 in his will "for the promotion of Agricultural or Horticultural improvements, or other Philosophical or Philanthropic purposes at their discretion." One of the trustees of the estate was Arnold's nephew, the private school headmaster George Berrell Emerson. Emerson decided it should be used to build an arboretum.

But even in the 1860s, the amount was too small to pay for an appropriate amount of land. Thus arose the first innovative idea: to build an arboretum on a portion of the Bussey land—finally relinquished by his heirs—and plant and maintain it with the interest from the Arnold money.

Gray, who by now was determined to see his tree collection built before he retired, agreed. The problem seemed resolved with the appointment of Charles Sprague Sargent *(see sidebar, page 96)* as Arnold Professor of Dendrology and director of the newly designated Arnold Arboretum in the spring of 1872. He was to grow "all the trees, shrubs and herbaceous plants, either indigenous or exotic, which can be

raised in the open air at the said West Roxbury."

One of the three ponds in the Arboretum. All are located near the Bradley Collection of Rosaceous Plants.

Pursuing the Dream

Sargent, a lackluster student who graduated from Harvard 88th in a class of 90, had no horticultural experience except as manager of his father's estate in Brookline. Outside of his military service, he had never held a job. Arnold's bequest would generate less than $3,000 a year to turn what he considered "a worn-out farm" into a botanic study ground.

But Sargent did have two things on his side: He was stubborn, and he could use his connections to bring in money, expertise, and political backing.

First, through mutual friends, he enlisted the help of Frederick Law Olmsted. Olmsted agreed to lay out the arboretum gratis as long as Sargent paid expenses. Sargent concurred, taking money from his own pocket and raising the rest from friends. Even so, he knew he couldn't build the roads and pathways and maintain the arboretum with the budget he'd been given.

By now, plans for Boston's "pleasure parks," referred to later as the Emerald Necklace, were under way,

inspiring Sargent to come up with the idea of having the city underwrite his costs in exchange for public access to the arboretum. As he envisioned it, the city would buy the land and lease it back to Harvard, which would keep control of the collections. "It is a capital bargain for both parties," said Olmsted, who saw a chance to vastly increase the spread of his parks.

But neither Harvard president Charles Eliot nor members of the city council wanted to do business with the other. "The sole difficulty is that nobody is alive to the opportunity," Olmsted, disappointed, confided to a friend.

It was four years before negotiations even began; they would drag on for another four. Even after the city council voted formally to turn him down, Sargent persisted. He hired one of Eliot's sons as an apprentice, and he organized an Arboretum Committee of the city's most prominent residents, more than 1,300 of whom signed a petition in his support.

Another city council vote was

Charles Sprague Sargent
The Force Behind the Arnold Arboretum

The man most responsible for America's first successful public arboretum is often said to have created it through sheer force of will. He had little else to work with.

Charles Sprague Sargent, who had no scientific training in botany, was given what he called a "worn-out farm" and a modest bequest to staff, design, and plant his "garden of trees." There was lukewarm support from Harvard University, which owned the land, and many Boston city leaders wanted nothing to do with the idea.

But Sargent was wealthy and extremely well-connected. He would stubbornly persist in building his beloved arboretum, which he would run (or, more accurately, refuse to relinquish) for more than half a century.

Son of a prominent Beacon Hill banker and financier, Sargent was born in 1841 into a family that included a chief justice, the founder of Universalism in America, and the painter John Singer Sargent. Another relative, Francis W. Sargent, later was elected governor of Massachusetts. But Sargent himself did little in his early life to hint of the accomplishment to come. He served in the Union Army during the Civil War and, after an obligatory trip to Europe, returned in 1869, when he was 27. But he did not go into banking like his father. He didn't take any job at all, save managing his father's 22-acre Brookline garden estate, Holm Lea.

Here, finally, was something that held Sargent's interest. Holm Lea was crossed by ingeniously laid-out tree-covered paths lined with shrubs, and boasted formidable collections of laurels and rhododendrons. Sargent gained extensive experience in horticulture while managing the property. In the spring of 1872, thanks in large part to family connections, he was named director of Harvard's botanic garden in Cambridge.

The university's garden was comparatively tiny—barely seven acres—and exhibited only herbaceous plants. Sargent had bigger things in mind. Connections quickly came in handy once again when his cousin, George Barrell Emerson, was named as a trustee of the estate of amateur gardener and wealthy merchant James Arnold, who had left just under $104,000 "for the promotion of Agricultural or Horticultural improvements, or other Philosophical or Philanthropic purposes at their discretion." Harvard also owned a farm in the Jamaica Plain section, left to it by Benjamin Bussey, another gentleman farmer. Why couldn't the university build an arboretum there with Arnold's money?

There were plenty of good reasons. For one, the proceeds of the Arnold bequest would generate only $3,000 a year to turn the Bussey farm into an arboretum, and pay the salaries of its staff. For another, few, including Sargent, were even sure they knew what an arboretum was.

Undeterred, Sargent enlisted the support of Frederick Law Olmsted, who he convinced to help design the site at cost; Sargent would pay the expenses out of his own pocket and by using contributions from his friends. Since the arboretum site lay in the path of the nascent Emerald Necklace, he proposed a partnership with the city's parks department. But Harvard president Charles Eliot was reluctant to give up any power over the parcel, and members of the city council opposed helping Harvard build its forest.

Sargent schemed, plotted, and negotiated. He lined up support from 1,305 of Boston's leading residents, many of them relatives or close friends. They formed an "Arboretum Committee" and signed a petition in support of the idea. Among the signers: the city's top businessmen, ex-mayors, and ex-governors. "The petition would be a prize to a collector of autographs," one newspaper wrote. Finally, at the end of 1882, all the parties agreed. The city bought the land from Harvard and leased it back for a dollar a year for 1,000 years. Harvard, in return, agreed to keep it open to the public. Taxpayers also picked up the bill for preparing the grounds, building roads and footpaths, and providing police patrols.

Finally, Sargent could apply his considerable energies to laying out the arboretum, which slowly took shape over 25 years. He spent some of his own wealth to supplement

Charles Sprague Sargent sitting at his desk in the library of the Hunnewell administration building, c. 1904

the Arnold income. He arranged exchanges of trees and plants with privately owned collections, and with England's famous Kew Gardens and other gardens in Europe. He led expeditions across the country and around the world in search of still more specimens. An ardent early conservationist, he was instrumental in preserving much of the Adirondack forests. He inherited his cherished Holm Lea from his father and cultivated and maintained it as his own personal sanctuary. And while his headstrong nature would continue to put him at odds with other scientists, it also helped him build a collection of 6,000 species and varieties of trees and shrubs in the 55 years he ran the arboretum— 1,932 of them the first of their kind in the United States. A subsequent director, with typical Harvard understatement, called Sargent "fortunate." This successor wrote: "He had authority and isolation, qualified friends for counsel, private personal funds and friends who could help financially, and only the restriction of space and climate for the types of plants he wanted to grow.

During his tenure, the arboretum would be described as a one-man institution.

Sargent's 14-volume catalogue of trees, *The Silva of North America,* which took him 20 years to finish, is still considered an important work. But Sargent didn't succeed at everything. He vastly overestimated the number of varieties of the hawthorn, a thorny plant categorized by its Latin name, Crataegus. He listed 700 different species and 22 varieties of crataegus, which turned out to be wrong by a factor of almost ten. Other botanists mocked the error and derided Sargent's expertise.

Sargent outlived many of his critics. He was still director of his "garden of trees" when he died at 85 in 1927 of intestinal flu. He left $30,000 to the arboretum, $10,000 of which was to accumulate for 100 years. That bequest is estimated to be worth $100 million on its maturity. His estate, Holm Lea, however, was sold off and subdivided into house lots.

The Forest Hills Gate is one of five "handsome and substantial iron gates" that Charles Sprague Sargent reported had been installed by 1899. Two more entrances, on the Peters Hill extension, were added the following year.

held, and this time Sargent's proposal prevailed. A year later, after all the details had been hammered out, the city agreed to buy the land and lease it to the university for 1,000 years at $1 a year beginning in 1883. It would also pay for roads, paths, and boundary fences, and provide police protection. Harvard would hire and pay the arboretum's staff and oversee its scientific operations, and the tree collection would stay open to the public free of charge. Under the arrangement, the city built three and a half miles of roads, six miles of footpaths, and seven gated entrances over 25 years. In 1894, it would accept another 67 acres—the adjacent Peters Hill tract—as an addition to the original agreement. In addition to permanent free public access, taxpayers got a sliver of the property for a new parkway, the Arborway. The arboretum would become the first in America planned from the outset to be opened to the public.

Design and Construction

Olmsted laid out the paths and roads in the "picturesque" style that prevailed in his other parks, but he and Sargent also opted to arrange the plant collections in botanical sequence by family and genus, with related species planted together, under the Bentham and Hooker system of classification then in vogue. It was to be the living museum that Emerson and others had proposed. "A visitor driving through the arboretum will be able to obtain a general idea of the arborescent vegetation of the north temperate zone without even leaving his carriage," Sargent boasted. "It is hoped that

such an arrangement, while avoiding the stiff and formal lines of the conventional botanic garden, will facilitate the comprehensive study of the collections, both in their scientific and picturesque aspects." Olmsted considered the arboretum truer to his original design than any of his other parks.

Sargent, meanwhile, set out to plant every woody plant that could live outdoors in the New England climate. This would be "much the best arboretum in the world," as the almost exuberant Olmsted put it.

Despite the arboretum's paltry budget, exchanges were agreed to with privately owned collections and with Kew and other gardens in Europe. In 1892, an administration building was added, underwritten by Sargent's friend H. H. Hunnewell. (It was renovated in 1993.) Within 25 years, the roads were finished. Within 50, there were thousands of species and varieties of shrubs and trees being grown in the arboretum. There are now 4,371, including 1,932 introduced there for the first time in the United States. There were also 909,000 specimens in the herbarium. Today, there are 1.5 million.

"The arboretum has lost no opportunity to increase the number of species of plants" in its collection, Sargent wrote around the time of the arboretum's 50th anniversary. "Its officers and agents have continued to explore the forests of North America; they have visited every country in Europe, the Caucasus, Eastern Siberia, and Korea, and have studied every species of tree growing in the forests of the Japanese Empire. Agents of the arboretum have visited the Malay Peninsula, Java, the Himalayas, the high mountains of east tropical Africa, southern Africa, Australia, Mexico, Peru, Chile, southward to Tierra del Fuego and the Falkland Islands."

Yesterday and Tomorrow

There have been milestones since Sargent's death in 1927. In 1938, a hurricane badly damaged the collection. In 1942, the arboretum added the 150-acre Case Estate in suburban Weston, which is used as an experimental garden. Part of the herbarium was removed to Harvard's Cambridge campus in 1954, but new greenhouses were added in Jamaica Plain in 1962. A bonsai collection was contributed in 1937, a garden of rosaceous plants in 1985. Collecting expeditions have also continued, with seven major collecting trips to Asia since 1977.

But an arboretum, by definition, generally changes at the slow pace of its plants and trees—that is, imperceptibly. "The Arnold Arboretum is not a school of forestry or of landscape gardening," Sargent said. "It is a station for the study of trees as individuals in their scientific relations, economic properties, and cultural requirements and possibilities. It has been managed not merely as a New England museum, but as a national and international institution working to increase knowledge

Construction of Meadow Road, c. 1892. A derrick, center, is being used to lift stones for a culvert to carry water under the roadway. The newly finished administration building is seen at right.

of trees in all parts of the world and as anxious to help a student in Tasmania or New Caledonia as in Massachusetts."

The arboretum now has an operating budget of $6.5 million a year.

 # A Walking Tour of the Arnold Arboretum

Its Bentham and Hooker classification system, and the ubiquitous labels make the arboretum easy on the visitor. Families of plants and trees are grouped together in botanical sequence, beginning with magnolias at the Arborway Gate, and ending with conifers at the Walter Street Gate. Almost all the trees are labeled, and the shrubs and bushes are tagged with cards that give their scientific and common names and origins. Even the little witch hazel on the paths is catalogued. "Information is here administered so delightfully that one is hardly conscious of being at school," botanist M. C. Robbins wrote. Lessons aside, the tree-covered paths wind through wooded knolls, open meadows, hills and valleys, and past ponds, cliffs, and a stream called Bussey Brook. Keep in mind that traversing the property on the main route alone, without detouring onto any other trails, is about a four-mile round trip.

The arboretum now comprises 265 acres bordered by Centre Street, Walter Street, and the Arborway, with almost 13,000 specimens of living plants and trees. Its collection emphasizes the woody species of North America and eastern Asia that can survive the cold-weather climate; beeches, honeysuckles,

magnolias, crabapples, oaks, rhododendrons, and lilacs are particularly well-represented.

Venerable and Exotic Trees

A good place to begin a visit is in the Hunnewell Building just inside the Arborway gate, where a permanent exhibit tells the story of the arboretum and includes a 9-by-15-foot scale model of the landscape. On the gate itself is a plaque that dedicates the park to Sargent. The arboretum, it says—with perhaps a touch more

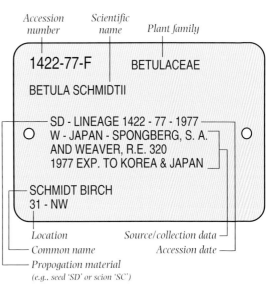

The 4,500 kinds of woody plants cultivated in the Arboretum's collections are grouped together by plant family for easy comparison. These groups are arranged in a botanical sequence along the main drive. Each plant is labeled with its scientific and common name, its country of origin, and an accession number that links the plant to its permanent, computer-stored record.

Accession number
Scientific name
Plant family

1422-77-F   BETULACEAE

BETULA SCHMIDTII

SD - LINEAGE 1422 - 77 - 1977
W - JAPAN - SPONGBERG, S. A.
AND WEAVER, R.E. 320
1977 EXP. TO KOREA & JAPAN

SCHMIDT BIRCH
31 - NW

Location
Source/collection data
Common name
Accession date
Propagation material
(e.g., seed 'SD' or scion 'SC')

Magnolias are among the oldest flowering plants on earth. It's believed that they evolved their large-petaled flowers specifically to attract the beetles that were once the primary insect pollinators. Magnolia "Randy" blossoms are pictured at right.

credit than Olmsted, Emerson, Arnold, Bussey, Eliot, and others would have conceded—was "his creation (and) is a living and enduring memorial." On the other side is a plaque noting that Mr. Sargent's tree garden has been named a national historic landmark.

To the right of the gate is a cucumber magnolia planted in 1880, one of an estimated 600 trees inside the arboretum that are more than 100 years old. The name of this magnolia refers to the shape of its fruit, which is red but cucumber-shaped. Another centenarian tree comes a little further along, where the path diverges from the Meadow Road on the right: a tulip tree planted here in 1894 and now 90 feet tall. Among the tallest types of trees in North America, tulip trees are named for their tulip-shaped flowers, which endure through the cold of the winter. These trees can grow to more than twice this size, though their straight trunks have made them victim to lumber operations since the days when Native Americans and early settlers cut them down to make dugout canoes.

A tree with an even more interesting story also appears here. It's a metasequoia, a relative of the California redwood, found in China and planted here in 1948, long after it was believed to be extinct. It's recognizable by its needlelike leaves.

On the left is a scene out of an English landscape painting: a forest

A purple beech tree in full form

Arnold Arboretum Bloom Calendar

Getting the most out of the arboretum is as dependent on the season as it is the map. Along with the lilacs, colorful crabapples, forsythias, magnolias, dogwoods, and azaleas bloom in the spring; flame azaleas, dogwoods, hydrangeas, and rhododendrons in the summer. In the fall, the foliage of 130 different types of maples sets the scenery ablaze with color, and acorns and fallen leaves crunch underfoot. The winter landscape is a show of conifers and hollies.

Here is the arboretum's calendar of natural events:

March
Hazels, pussy willows, witch hazels

April
Andromedas, cornelian cherries, daphnes, forsythias, honeysuckles, early magnolias, red maples, rhododendron, shadbushes, witch hazels

May
Azaleas (Ghent, pinkshell, royal, torch), brooms, cherries, cotoneasters, crabapples, currants, flowering dogwoods, dove tree, enkianthus, hawthorns, honeysuckles, horse chestnuts, lilacs, American magnolias, saucer magnolias, mountain ashes, pears, flowering quinces, redbuds, silverbells, early spireas, tree peonies, viburnums, wisterias

Flowering quince and rhododendron (left) both bloom in April.

Tree peonies flower for several weeks.

June
Azaleas (flame), beautybushes,
catalpas, deutzias, kousa dogwoods,
fringe trees, climbing hydrangeas,
late lilacs, sweetbay magnolias,
mock oranges, mountain laurels,
catawba rhododendron, roses,
tulip trees, weigelas, yellowwoods,
zenobias

July
Azaleas (summer), bottlebrush
buckeyes, buttonbushes, castor
aralias, clethras, goldenrain trees,
hydrangea, hypericums, lindens,
silk trees, sourwoods, stewartias,
yuccas

August
Aralias, harlequin glorybowers,
hibiscus, late hydrangea, pagoda
trees

*Wisteria blooms are short-lived
but wonderfully fragrant.*

September
Sweet autumn clematis, franklinias,
fall foliage begins

October and November
Native witch hazels, fall foliage

December and January
Conifers, hollies, ghost brambles,
trees with exfoliating bark

*The delicate blooms of the weeping higan
tree are a harbinger of spring.*

of willows across a meadow of reeds and marsh grasses called, not coincidentally, the Meadow. (To see these from the opposite perspective, follow Willow Path, which runs just inside the wall dividing the arboretum from the Arborway.) Closer to Meadow Road you'll find a massive silver maple that dates from 1881, identifiable by its bright green leaves with silvery undersides, which turn yellow in the fall. Silver maples can grow as much as 50 feet in 20 years. At 120 feet, this one is the tallest tree in the arboretum. This species can

also produce a high quality maple syrup.

Also on the left is a Lavalle cork tree, native to central Japan, whose bark is crisscrossed like the brickwork of a Gothic chapel, and whose gnarled roots spread along the ground. There are variations of this species on both sides of the road, though this one is the most remarkable. Compare it to the American basswood opposite, a comparatively nondescript tree with a straight and simple trunk, often found in the oak and hickory forests of the south-

Azaleas form a highly colorful display of bloom in the springtime, but many varieties commonly grown in the south are not hardy in the northeast. Ghent azaleas (insets) are very popular, and many appealing forms are available.

Reeds, marsh grasses, and willows on the Meadow create an enchanting scene reminiscent of an English landscape.

ern Appalachians. We've now entered the arboretum's North Woods.

There are also interesting shrubs here, including a Korean flatpine prickly ash, whose thin branches have exotic thorns; and a common smoke tree, a shrub native to Europe and Asia that grows to about 15 feet. Smoke trees have yellow wood, and fruit that ends in a downy sort of hair that looks like smoke protruding from its branches. Also on the left are painted maples, natives to eastern Asia, which twist as they grow, and whose branches spread into a canopy of leaves.

Native Trees
On the right at the top of a small hill are trees native to the eastern United States, including large sugar maples and black locusts. Tapped for their syrup, sugar maples can produce as much as 60 gallons of sap per year. It takes about 32 gallons of sap to make one gallon of syrup. These trees are also in demand for their wood, thanks to the varied patterns of their grain. They grow to a height of 100 feet, with bark that is rough and scaly, and leaves that turn a brilliant orange and yellow in the fall. The black locusts have a comparatively crooked trunk and irregular crown, and grow to between 40 and 80 feet with deeply furrowed bark. The wood from this type of tree was used by early colonists for timber. Not all the trees on this low hill are common. There is an exotic Kentucky coffee tree along the road. These short-trunked trees can reach a height of 100 feet.

Azaleas
Farther along and on the left are the azaleas—pinkshell, royal, torch, Ghent, and other varieties, which bloom in mid- to late May and, in some cases, early July. Azaleas are shrubs with clusters of vase-shaped orange, red, or yellow flowers. Royal azaleas reach a height of 10 feet, with pink flowers two and a half inches wide; torch azaleas grow to eight feet, with red flowers two inches wide. One kind of azalea, the honeysuckle, can be spotted by the spreading branches that form the rounded shape of this shrub. It

Horse chestnuts and buckeyes (as the nuts too are called) somewhat resemble American chestnuts in appearance. But the true chestnut is virtually extinct, a result of a fungus that eradicated most of the species by the early 20th century. The fruit of horse chestnuts is very bitter and is edible only after careful preparation.

Also called the American basswood, the linden has heart-shaped leaves, and slender leaflike bracts that in early summer produce a profusion of yellowish flowers with a sweet, fragrant scent.

Buckeyes, left, are of the same genus as the horse chestnut. Their fruit, with its eyelike markings, is still carried as charms by some rural people. Ohio is called the Buckeye State because of the prevalence of the Ohio buckeye.

Dogwood blossoms are actually an inconspicuous flower surrounded by large, showy bracts which are often mistaken for its petals. Dogwood anthracnose, a fungal disease, has killed many wild woodland dogwoods since the 1980s.

Oaks have proven to be resistant to the diseases that have ravaged other native hardwoods and are among the longest lived—some have been known to survive for 600 years.

blooms with creamy white flowers and colorful, fragrant fruit that attracts birds.

Eleanor Cabot Bradley Collection of Rosaceous Plants

Just past the azaleas and beyond a small still pond filled with water lilies is the Eleanor Cabot Bradley Collection of Rosaceous Plants, a seven-acre section opened formally in 1985. The collection was designed to reflect Frederick Law Olmsted's naturalistic design principles. Here grass paths wind among 3,000 different species of the rose family, very few of which look as visitors expect, including many with edible fruits. What they have in common are flowers with five petals, and, in many cases, thorns of various size and sharpness.

Not even the garden roses in this maze-like section look much like their cultivated counterparts sold commercially or grown for prizes. The Duchesse de Montebello, for example, which was raised by benefactor Bradley herself in her garden in Canton, Massachusetts, has a small pink flower and stems almost without thorns. There is

also an exotic leatherleaf rose with thorny branches, grown on Sargent's estate of Holm Lea; an Alabama snow-wreath that blooms into feathery white flowers with no petals and is found naturally only in Alabama; the Scarlet Meidiland, a shrub with tiny scarlet roses, and which flowers well into the fall; and the Japanese *Malus sieboldii* tree, which sprouts not only whitish-pink flowers but also yellow-orange–colored crabapples. Also watch for the flowering quince, a shrub about five feet high with dark green foliage, nearly thornless brambles of branches, and fluffy flowers that range in hue from pink to tomato red when they bloom in early May. To enjoy all this beauty, look for the stone bench set in a peaceful spot overlooking the rose garden, though it's

Forsythias are prized in those regions of the country where their early spring flowers lend conspicuous color to gardens that have been dormant over the winter. This large specimen can be found at the foot of Bussey Hill Road.

hard to find. Search out the weathered post-and-rail fence above it, and behind that, a towering white oak.

Here the road recoils from the unwelcome intrusion of a high-rise that houses the offices of the state Department of Public Health and begins to slope up Bussey Hill. On a connecting path that serves as a shortcut is a yellowwood planted in 1881. Though native to the southeastern United States, the yellowwood can survive temperatures as cold as 30 degrees below zero. Its leaves change color not in the fall but in the spring, to yellowish green and then to green, before sprouting white, fragrant flowers in late May. The tree gets its name from the yellow color of its wood when cut. There are also locust trees here, including a giant honey locust with a thick mane of leaves, just at the point where the road turns.

Forsythia Collection

With the high-rise in front of you, turn right and look for the narrow trail to the left. This will take you to the forsythia collection, one of the less well-known prizes of the arboretum's cultivated plants. The Arnold Arboretum serves as the international registration authority for forsythias, and boasted some of the first species of these Asian plants to reach the United States. They were brought by Ernest Henry Wilson, who succeeded Charles Sprague Sargent in 1927, and who personally led countless expeditions to the East. The Korean forsythia Wilson imported to the arboretum was particularly hardy, and was used to develop forsythias that could survive in colder climates. Many of those are

The Rosaceae are a large family of plants, characterized by showy flowers with five separated petals and numerous stamens borne on the margin of a cup-like structure. They include important fruit plants such as the apple, cherry, peach, pear, plum, raspberry, and strawberry, as well as ornamentals such as the rose, flowering quince (inset), and spirea (left).

here, their shrubby limbs creeping along the ground. The bell-shaped, greenish-yellow flowers bloom in early spring.

The Lilac Collection

As the road (here called Bussey Hill Road) circles gently to the top of Bussey Hill, it passes the famous lilac collection, the second-largest in North America, and one of the most popular sections of the park. There are almost 500 lilac plants of about 250 different types, including 190 cultivated for their size and color and characterized by their small clusters of bright and fragrant flowers. They scent the entire arboretum for five weeks every spring, including Lilac Sunday, when as many as 30,000 people visit. It's also the only day of the year when picnics are allowed inside the arboretum. In the early part of the 20th century, extra police had to be called in to control the crowds.

Catalpas form a backdrop for the lilacs. These trees, distinctive for their reddish-brown bark and stout, irregularly shaped branches, have large leaves. In the spring clusters of large white flowers with yellow stripes appear; in the fall, they produce a narrow, cylindrical fruit.

There are also interesting distractions on the right, including a Korean linden bush with bright red berries, and a Chinese pagoda tree,

the ends of whose branches hang so low, it's easy to mistake it for a shrub. Just beyond is a shady grove of tall sassafras trees, whose patterned bark recalls the cork trees near the entrance. Oil from this fragrant tree has traditionally been used to perfume soap, make tea, and flavor root beer. Contrast these with the smooth-barked, thick-trunked Asian elms that come up next.

At the fork where a spur of the main road diverges toward the Dana Greenhouses are viburnums, shrubs from five to eight feet in height whose dark leaves turn purple in the fall and whose fragrant white flowers bloom in May and June. The greenhouses were completed in 1962 and total 3,744 square feet. They are not open to the public.

Larz Anderson Bonsai Collection

Also in the greenhouse complex is the Bonsai House, where the Larz Anderson Bonsai Collection is displayed from mid-April to mid-November. Bonsai, or dwarf plants grown in containers, is an ancient art form practiced in China and Japan for more than 1,000 years. These specimens are kept in cold storage at temperatures just above

freezing in the winter. The large hinoki cypresses, imported from Japan in 1913, are the oldest living bonsais known to exist in the United States. Bonsai trees require an extraordinary amount of care, including repeated pruning of both branches and roots to maintain their shape and compactness, shaping with copper or aluminum wire, frequent watering , addition of fertilizer every two weeks, and constant attention to temperature and humidity.

A collection of sun-loving shrubs

The famous paper, or canoe, birch of the northern United States and Canada has bark which separates in layers and was used by Native Americans for canoes and baskets. The birch's catkin, inset, is a tassellike flower cluster that is either staminate (male, producing pollen) or pistillate (female, producing seeds).

and vines is also planned to open here in the spring of 2002, including climbing vines draped over high frames, all displayed in neat rows divided by low stone walls.

Bussey Hill

Some of the original tree plantings in the arboretum are located on the sparsely planted lawn on the left that leads up to the top of Bussey Hill, where beeches, ashes, elms, and hick-

We can thank Frederick Law Olmsted for the lilac display. Director Charles Sprague Sargent didn't think lilacs deserved prominent placement on the property, but Olmsted successfully argued that they would be popular with the public. The Arboretum's collection is particularly appreciated on Lilac Sunday.

The multitude of different tree types and woody plants attracts birds throughout the year. Nearly 150 species of birds have been sighted in the Arboretum.

ories are located. There are several kinds of brilliantly white-barked birches, including paper birches brought from central North America, and European white birches. Their fate is uncertain. Their New England cousins are dying off from disease, and several of these trees may not last. There also is an interesting black cherry tree here, with a fat trunk and a cherry smell. It produces its dark red cherries in late summer. On the right as the road slowly curves are plane trees, commonly known as sycamore or buttonwood, whose hard lumber is popular for furniture including butcher blocks.

The Mighty Oaks

Take a shortcut up the stairs to the summit to see the oaks. These trees are as sturdy as the birches are frail, with broad trunks and strong, graceful branches. The pin oak here is named for its short twigs and pinlike spurs; the red oak for its leaves that turn dark red in the fall. The bur oak, also found here, is distinguished by its almost perfect oval spread. There's a particularly proud northern red oak on the right as the road hooks to the top of the hill, where there are unimpeded views to the southwest, and a fresh-smelling copse of eastern white pines—evergreens with horizontal branches and blue-green needles. The straight, tall trunks of these trees, which can grow to a height of 100 feet, were once used for ships' masts and are still in demand for millwork, trim, and pulpwood. The eastern white pine is the state tree of Maine—the Pine Tree State.

Double back down the hill past the oaks and into the elms for an outstanding view of the Boston skyline. Now return to the main road. On the right are silverbells, trees that got their name from their bell-like white to pale pink flowers, which emerge in late April and early May.

There are more oaks on the left, including huge ivy-covered black oaks that shoot straight to the sky before opening their branches, handsome steel-straight bur oaks, and swamp white oaks. At the one-

mile marker on the right is exposed rock where the striations of a glacier still can be seen.

The Conifers

Here is the beginning of the arboretum's vast conifer collection of spruces, larches, firs, and pines, beginning with a Canadian hemlock, a dwarf white spruce, and a ghostly cedar of Lebanon. There is a trail cutting through the conifers, called Conifer Path, which is a good route for the return trip; it connects the Walter Street Gate with Bussey Hill, and lets you see more of these trees up close. (After returning from Peters Hill, detour over the bridge across shallow Bussey Brook into the evergreens.)

The word conifer comes from the Latin word for "cone-bearing," though some conifers produce a berrylike fruit and not cones. Most also have in common

Bleeding hearts, above, and catalpa blossoms, right, add springtime color to Bussey Hill. Catalpa wood is very durable in contact with soil. About 90 percent of all catalpa cut is made into fence posts.

A small footbridge crosses Bussey Brook where it joins Spring Brook at the foot of Hemlock Hill Road.

Left, a weeping European larch will make a dense ground cover if allowed to sprawl. Below, wildflowers brighten Conifer Path, a less-traveled route that runs through the Central Woods.

Unlike most other fir trees, larches are deciduous conifers—that is, they lose their leaves at the end of the growing season. They are also part of a group of plants called gymnosperms, meaning their seeds are born openly in cones.

These evergreen trees are commonly known as hemlock or hemlock spruce. They can be distinguished from other conifers—cone-bearing trees—by their flat, linear, leaves, which have two long, whitish lines on their lower surfaces. The bark is high in tannic acid, useful in the process of tanning hides.

Englemann spruces, above, are very long-lived. One Colorado specimen was determined to be 852 years old. The Nikko fir, right, is a variety belonging to the conifer family. They are valued for planting as lawn ornaments. Firs may be distinguished from spruces by their standing cones, while cones of the Spruce are pendant.

their needle-shaped leaves, which they keep throughout the winter. The hemlock is the quintessential conical-topped pine, with slender branches that often droop to the ground and are a favorite food of white-tailed deer. The white spruce is taller and thinner, its lowest branches beginning higher off the ground. The mournful-looking shrublike cedar of Lebanon has "weeping" branches and blue needles.

At the next turn in the road, the forest thickens into still more pungent pines along a hilly section of the arboretum that smells like Christmas. This is the quietest part of the park, where bird songs mask the traffic noise. Here are hundreds more hemlocks—so thick that the light can barely pierce their branches—and mountain laurels, small trees that form thickets and flower with large, pink saucer-shaped clusters in the spring.

Go back up again to the curve in the road at the base of Bussey Hill. There are two other trails here worth taking. Follow Beech Path to the first—Chinese Path—which leads back up the hill and takes you past some of the many Asiatic trees and shrubs imported by the arboretum in the early 1900s, including bam-

The two dove trees at the Arboretum are rare specimens. Native to China they are often the first examples of their type to be viewed by visiting botanists from that country.

boos, a silk tree, and a paperbark maple. Among the most interesting are the Stewartias, trees native to Japan and Korea with creamy white flowers and golden stamens whose blooms last only a day. The dark green leaves turn yellow, red, and purple in the fall. These trees were grown from seeds collected in Korea and Japan by Wilson in 1917. In the same section are Franklinias, fall-flowering American trees that no longer grow in the wild. The

The Linda J. Davison Rhododendron Path offers a springtime feast for the eyes. The genus Rhododendron, which also includes azaleas, is a member of the heath family (Ericaceae). The heath family includes the heaths and heathers, blueberries, mountain laurels, Pernettya, andromeda, and several other ornamental plant groups. More than a thousand species have been described within the genus Rhododendron.

Franklinias were discovered in Georgia in 1765 by the Philadelphia botanist John Bartram, who named them after Benjamin Franklin. Among those growing here are the two oldest in the world, dating from 1905. Their flowers, which look much like those of the Stewartias, bloom for a month or more.

Linda J. Davison Rhododendron Path

Retrace your steps along Beech Path again, to the intersection with the dirt and gravel Linda J. Davison Rhododendron Path. Rhododendrons are actually a genus of evergreen shrubs that includes the azaleas we saw earlier along the road. Their flowers are larger and bell-

Flowering cherries (right) and crabapples (above) are a favorite with visitors to the Arboretum. The Sargent cherry (Prunus sargentii) *was named after the Arboretum's first director. Crabapples are differentiated from apple trees based on their fruit size. If the fruit is two inches in diameter or less, it is termed a crabapple.*

shaped but equally colorful when they bloom in the spring. This path is also lined with Koyama spruce, a slow-growing evergreen from Asia that can reach 120 feet; white mulberry, a fruit-bearing tree with lobed leaves; narrow-leaf ash, a strong tree with small flowers; the spindly and descriptively named big-cone dragon spruce; and an enormous sweetgum tree, which grows commonly in the northeast.

Now head west again. Hemlock Hill is on your left; along the right side of the road runs Bussey Brook, and beyond it are more of the arboretum's many conifer trees. Here the main route changes its name to Hemlock Hill Road. This will take you to the Bussey Street Gate and, across busy Bussey Street itself, to the 67-acre Peters Hill, added by the city to the arboretum in 1894. But before leaving, stop to see the ginkgoes.

Ginkgo Trees

One of the oldest species of tree on earth, the ginkgo was common all over the globe 200 million years ago but now survives only as a single species native to China. Some paleobotanists believe it is the oldest living genus of plant. Along with its dis-

tinctive fan-shaped leaf, the ginkgo is perhaps best known for the malodorous flesh encasing the seeds the female trees produce each fall; though often erroneously called a fruit, it is in fact an aril, a fleshy seed coat. The seeds on the female tree look like apricots (*ginkgo* is the Chinese word for apricot), and the leaves turn yellow in the fall.

Lacy larch trees and more straight, tall pines stand sentinel at the gate to the South Woods, colloquially known as Peters Hill, where the trees are considerably younger and smaller. Some have only been planted in the last few decades. Hawthorns date from the early 1900s; a display of crabapples was planted in the 1950s. So close does the surrounding city press in at the edges of this newer section that some of the trees here overhang the neighbors' yards.

Peters Hill

Once past the gate, go right up the circular road to Peters Hill. Along the way are more exotic plantings, many from 20th-century specimen-collecting expeditions, including a Japanese black pine—a small, irregularly shaped tree that grows 35 feet tall but as much as 25 feet wide,

The honey locust is native to the eastern half of the United States but is planted as a shade tree in many regions of the country. It has heavily fragrant flowers attractive to bees, compound leaves made up of small leaflets, and large branching thorns. The pods, which usually twist with age, are brown, flat, and have a sweet, edible pulp that has been used to make beer.

Looking north from the top of 240-foot Peters Hill affords visitors a view of the entire arboretum below and the Boston skyline beyond.

with green, twisted needles seven inches long. This young tree looks like a single thick finger reaching from the ground. There is also a Japanese red pine, which despite its name turns yellow in the winter; a white fir, which defies the same sense of logic with its bluish leaves; an elegant Nikko fir, with neatly spaced branches and dense green needles; more Canadian hemlock; and Norway spruce, widely used as Christmas trees.

On the right is a historic burying ground that predates the arboretum, the Walter Street Burying Ground, opened in 1711 when there was a church and parsonage at this site. Many early settlers are buried here beneath the widely scattered gravestones. There is also a large tomb, the final resting place of

Revolutionary War soldiers who died of smallpox at a nearby military hospital.

The highlight of this section is windswept Peters Hill itself. At 240 feet, it is the highest point in the arboretum, with extraordinary views of the city to the north, including the gleaming gold dome of the State House—with the entire arboretum in the foreground. It's the perfect way to punctuate a visit.

The Arnold Arboretum is open daily from dawn to dusk. Winter weekend hours are 10 a.m. to 2 p.m., November 1 through March 1. The Hunnewell Building, which houses the permanent exhibit "Science in the Pleasure Ground," is open from 9 a.m. to 4 p.m., Monday through Friday, noon to 4 p.m. on weekends, and closed on holidays. There is no admission charge. The Larz Anderson Bonsai Collection is on display from mid-April to mid-November. Free tours are given on some Wednesdays and Saturdays.

For recorded tour information, call 617-524-1718, ext. 773.

The arboretum holds an annual plant sale in September.

The arboretum's address is 125 Arborway, Jamaica Plain. Phone: 617-524-1718.

How to Get to the Arboretum

By subway: Take the MBTA Orange Line or Bus 39 from Copley Square to Forest Hills Station. The Arboretum's Forest Hills gate is two blocks from the station along the Arborway.

By car: From Boston or Cambridge, take Storrow Drive to the Fenway/Park Drive exit and follow the signs to the Riverway. The Riverway becomes the Jamaica Way and then the Arborway. The arboretum is at the junction of the Arborway and Centre Street.

From the west, take Route 128 (I-95) to Route 9 East. Continue on Route 9 for seven miles to the Riverway in Brookline (Route 1 South), following the signs toward Dedham and Providence. Follow the signs to the arboretum at the junction of the Arborway and Centre Street.

From the south, take the Southeast Expressway (I-93) to Exit 11 (Granite Avenue/Ashmont) onto Route 203 West. Follow Route 203 through Dorchester and past Franklin Park. The arboretum will be on your left just beyond the Forest Hills MBTA station. Proceed to the rotary, turn left at the light and go all the way around the rotary, doubling back to Route 203. The main gate will be on your right.

Parking: Parking is available outside the main gate, along the Arborway, and around the arboretum's perimeter. No vehicles are allowed inside the arboretum except by permit for people with disabilities. For a permit, apply to the receptionist at the Hunnewell Building weekdays from 9 a.m. to 3 p.m.

BEYOND
THE
NECKLACE

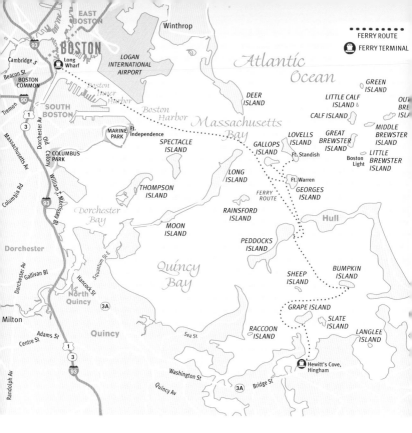

Boston Harbor Islands National Recreation Area

Boston's newest major park has proved a modern-day version of some of its oldest. It was reclaimed from a backdrop of pollution and neglect, and transports visitors from the commotion of the city to the peace and tranquillity of isolated open spaces, only moments from downtown.

But this time, the sanctuary is offshore. Officially known as the Boston Harbor Islands National Recreation Area, it's a sort of urban archipelago boasting ghosts, shipwrecks, buried treasure, secret passageways, forts, dungeons, and the nation's last manned offshore lighthouse; not to mention sandy ocean beaches, hik-

ing trails, isolated fishing spots and peaceful public campsites. Established as a national park in 1996, it totals 1,600 acres on 34 islands all within the C-shaped confines of the Greater Boston shoreline.

Boston has rediscovered the ocean that for centuries sustained it. Contamination has been flushed from Boston Harbor, named the nation's most polluted harbor in the 1980s. Popular commuter ferries cross from seaside suburbs to rejuvenated docks.

The murky, smelly veil that once hung over the harbor has been lifted to reveal again the watery tableau that is America's front yard.

At the end of the American Civil War, Confederate vice president Alexander Hamilton Stephens was imprisoned behind the 12-foot-thick granite walls of Fort Warren.

Georges Island

At the center of the harbor is Georges Island, where ferries from Long Wharf land. Smaller water taxis stand by to shuttle passengers to other islands. But Georges rates a lengthy visit in itself. It is home to one of the largest forts on the East Coast open to the public, the astonishingly well-preserved Civil War–era Fort Warren.

The star-shaped fort took more than 25 years to build, beginning in 1833, and its 12-foot-thick granite walls help account for its extraordinary endurance even in the face of previous neglect and vandalism. There are emplacements for 350 cannon, enlisted men's clubs, a semi-subterranean prison, underground passageways, a drawbridge, and a shot hoist elevator that could lift 1,000-pound rounds to elevated guns installed when ironclad ships came into service. Every August,

A harbor ferry approaches the landing at Georges Island. Behind the red-brick Visitor Center stand the walls of Fort Warren.

actors dressed as Union and Confederate soldiers set up camp and stage two days of convincing reenactments.

Fort Warren never fired its guns at an invading ship (although it once almost hit the Nantasket ferry accidentally during target practice). But more than 3,000 Confederates were imprisoned here, including Confederate vice president Alexander Hamilton Stephens. Political prisoners reportedly slept late, ate large lunches, smoked cigars, and took long strolls on the shoreline, while Union officers stationed on the island were credited with composing the lyrics to "John Brown's Body" in their ample leisure time.

Despite this lax pace, there were several executions at Fort Warren, including that of a prisoner's wife known only as the Woman in Black, who dressed as a man and smuggled herself onto the island in a bid to free her husband. Her last wish was to be hanged in women's clothing—black drapes from the mess hall fashioned into a crude dress. Since then, there have been more than 20 sightings of a ghostlike figure dressed in black; there are even court-martial records of sentries who shot at this apparition. An annual Halloween party is held at Fort Warren in her honor.

Here, too, is the best place to gaze admiringly at Boston Light, the quintessential lighthouse and the nation's oldest, on close-by Little Brewster Island. Manned by a crew of three coast guard keepers and their dog, the lighthouse is occasionally open to public tours. But it is best seen from the ocean-facing ramparts of Fort Warren. (For infor-

Boston Light, originally built in 1716, was America's first lighthouse. The lighthouse suffered damage during the Revolutionary War and required an extensive rebuilding in 1783.

mation about tours of Boston Light, call 617-740-4290).

The last stop is the lookout tower added during World War II to watch for submarines. It offers stunning views of Boston and, in late summer, unforgettable sunsets past the skyline to the west. You can see fish and birds in Boston Harbor, mostly cleaned now of its notorious pollution. On clear days, even far-off Salem and Cape Cod are visible. It's also a good place from which to map out expeditions to the other islands on the free water shuttles that leave from the Georges Island dock.

Lovells Island

The next stop, Lovells Island, has a history of shipwrecks, the most famous that of a packet ship from Maine that sank in a blizzard in 1786. With no shelter, all 13 passen-

Georges Island is significant largely for its strategic location, just south of the main ship channel in Boston Harbor. Besides historic Fort Warren, the island contains the park's visitors center, a large dock, picnic grounds, and a gravel beach pictured here.

gers and crew perished, including one young couple who froze in each other's arms against a rock. Still known as Lovers' Rock, the tragic spot is one of the most popular stops on the free tours. In 1782, the French man-of-war *Magnifique* went aground here, laden with gold coins that were never found and presumably are still buried. Lovells Island also has an underwater tunnel, a dubious submarine defense built so that explosives could be set beneath the harbor channel. It has never been used.

Lovells also has campsites and a beach with lifeguards. It's a perfect vantage point from which to watch as modern military, cruise, and cargo vessels and the occasional tall ship sail to or from the port, and aircraft make their descent to nearby Logan International Airport.

Peddocks Island

The largest island, Peddocks, also has a giant fort, but it's an eerie ruin, abandoned after World War II and overgrown with trees. Built in the 1890s, Fort Andrews housed artillery and, later, antiaircraft guns and observation stations. More than 1,000 Italian prisoners were held there during World War II. The small white wooden church beside the new $2 million pier was used by summer residents of the now abandoned cottage community that shared the island with the fort. One islander working in her garden found what turned out to be the remains of an Indian man who lived 4,100 years ago, the oldest skeleton ever discovered in New England.

The other islands housed reformatories, asylums, poorhouses, hospitals, prisons, barracks, and the homes of the eccentric rich. Atlantic Coast pirates hid out here, and it is on Gallops Island that the notorious Long Ben Avery was said to have buried his treasure. To warn off any more marauders, the townspeople left the bodies of captured pirates rotting in chains at the entrance to the harbor on Bird Island and on tiny Nix's Mate, now eroded to no more than a tidal flat marked with a stone.

Flora and Fauna of the Islands

Other than grass and sumac, there is little vegetation on the islands. Once they were covered with hemlock, maple, oak, pine, and hickory trees, but most of these were cut down for firewood or to create grazing pastures for cows and sheep. Aspens, pines, birches, and white poplars have grown, or are beginning to grow, in their place.

The new trees have provided nesting places for more than 100 bird species, including gulls, terns, herons, ducks, geese, hawks, plovers, sandpipers, doves, owls, woodpeckers, and perching birds. Shorebirds stop off along the mudflats of the harbor during their migration seasons, and hawks and songbirds can be found on several of the islands. There are also several rare or threatened species, including the barn owl, common tern, least tern, and northern harrier. As for

Peddocks Island has the longest shoreline of any island in Boston Harbor and is composed of four drumlins, or heads, connected by sand or gravel bars called tombolos.

land animals, there are cottontail rabbits, raccoons, skunks, gray squirrels, mice, muskrats, voles, Norway rats, and the occasional eastern garter, eastern smooth green, and northern brown snake.

As the harbor has been cleaned, sea grass and cordgrass have returned, and that has helped attract sea life. After cordgrasses die and decompose, they leave behind organic particles; these in turn are eaten by worms, mollusks, and crustaceans, which are eaten by fish. Boston Harbor is an estuary system where the Charles, Mystic, and Neponset rivers dump freshwater into salt water Massachusetts Bay. Along the rocky beaches of islands such as Peddocks there are lobsters, crabs, clams, and mussels. Striped bass, bluefish, and winter flounder swim offshore. Humpback, fin,

Beach grasses add a graceful touch to Bumpkin Island's shoreline. The island's slate and shell beaches and open fields are welcome retreats for city dwellers. The island also offers scenic vistas and three picnic areas.

sion charge for the islands or for Fort Warren on Georges Island. For information, call 617-223-8666.

Ferries to the Islands
Ferries to Georges Island operate weekends from Long Wharf in Boston (MBTA Aquarium station) between May and October and between 10 a.m. and 5:50 p.m. daily from late June through Labor Day. There is also daily summer ferry service from Hewitt's Cove in Hingham, departing at 10 a.m., 12:45 p.m., and 3:30 p.m., and returning at 11:15 a.m., 2 p.m., and 5 p.m. The round-trip fare is $8 for adults, $6 for seniors, and $4 for children ages 4–12. Call 617-227-4321.

From Georges Island, there are free water shuttles to Lovells, Peddocks, Gallops, Grape, and Bumpkin islands.

Ferries are wheelchair accessible, though debarking may be difficult. George's Island has some areas suitable for wheelchair use.

How to Get to the Ferries
By subway: Take the MBTA Blue Line to Aquarium Station and board ferries at Long Wharf. To Hewitt's Cove in Hingham, take the Red Line to Quincy Center and Bus 220 to the Hingham Shipyard.

By car: From the west, take the Massachusetts Turnpike to I-93 north and exit at Atlantic Avenue. From the south, take the Southeast Expressway (I-93) to the Atlantic Avenue exit. From the north, take I-93 to Exit 24 (Callahan Tunnel) and follow the signs to the New England Aquarium.

To Hewitt's Cove in Hingham, take Route 3A and follow the signs to the Hingham Shipyard.

Parking: Parking is extremely limited along the Boston waterfront on weekdays, when parking garages fill relatively early in the day. Parking rates are also very high. There is ample parking at Hewitt's Cove.

minke, and North Atlantic right whales can occasionally be seen as they travel between their feeding grounds. So can harbor porpoises and white-sided and striped dolphins.

Camping on the Islands
Campsites are available on several of the islands, where the peace and quiet is broken only by the gentle lapping of the waves against the shore. It's also possible to see the harbor under moonlight on a dinner cruise aboard one of the sleek megayachts that operate in the spring, summer, and early fall, carrying as many as 700 people in climate-controlled comfort with the city in shimmering sight but still out of earshot. The only noise is the sound of the live dance bands on the boats.

Camping is available on Lovells, Peddocks, Grape, and Bumpkin islands. A permit is required. Call 617-727-7676. Visitors should bring bottled water, as there is no freshwater on any of the islands except Georges. Bathroom facilities are available and there are picnic areas on Georges, Lovells, Gallops, Peddocks, Bumpkin, and Grape islands. There is a snack bar on Georges Island. Fishing is allowed.

The Boston Harbor Islands National Recreation Area is open from 9 a.m. to sunset from early May to mid-October. There is no admis-

Boston's Beaches

In the 1940s and '50s, Boston residents flocked to beaches in their neighborhoods. Children splashed in the water for relief from the heat. Parents dozed in the sand. Hawkers sold ice cream.

But many of these families left during an era of suburban flight. Urban beaches were neglected, low priorities in the competition for dwindling public funds. Racial discord found its way to the oceanfront in insular disputes that pitted neighborhoods against each other. Three hundred and fifty years of dumping sewage straight into the ocean left Boston Harbor more polluted than almost any other stretch of American coastline. The ocean just offshore became a smelly muck, dangerous even for wading. By 1985, the water at Constitution Beach met minimum federal swimming standards less than half the time.

Billions of dollars later, the harbor is so clean that Constitution Beach is safe for swimming more than 90 percent of the time. Dolphins, loons, and seals have returned. And millions more have been spent restoring Boston's beaches, with thousands of tons of fresh sand, new boardwalks and bathhouses, even retro nautical-themed light posts and benches.

Beachgoers have also rediscovered Boston's coastline. Fourteen beaches comprising 28 miles of coast have been restored, from Winthrop in the north to the Wollaston section of Quincy to the south. (Swimming also is allowed at beaches on Gallops, Grape, Bumpkin, Lovells, and Peddocks islands in the Boston Harbor Islands National Recreation Area.)

There are also plans for a "sapphire necklace," a 49-mile Harbor-Walk of connected paths and trails from Dorchester to East Boston, stretches of which have already been built as a sort of seaside counterpart to the Emerald Necklace. There's a bicycle path from South Boston to Dorchester, for example, with occasional granite stanchions that tell tales of the sea—the story of the *Magnifique*, for instance, a 74-gun French man-of-war that went aground in 1782. Desperate to prevent a rift with their only major ally, the Americans presented France with the 74-gun USS *America* as compensation, even though the *America* had been promised to John Paul Jones, the new nation's greatest naval hero, who angrily resigned.

Most Boston beaches are managed by the Metropolitan District Commission. For beach information, call 617-727-5250. For updated water quality information, call 617-727-5264 or check www.tbha.org/boston.htm.

Savin Hill and Malibu beaches (Dorchester Shores), Dorchester

Along and beyond the mouth of the Neponset River, the MDC's Malibu Beach offers protected swimming, while adjacent Savin Hill Beach, managed by the city of Boston, has swimming from a small beach about 1,000 feet long and 75 feet wide at high tide. Savin Hill Beach also features baseball fields and a tot lot. These were among the most popular Boston beaches in the mid-20th century, but were virtually abandoned by the 1990s. They have been revived with several thousand tons of sand, a concrete promenade, and amenities including nautical-style bollards and chains, distinctive light posts, and hardwood benches with art deco wrought-iron arms inspired by the fashion of the 1939 New York World's Fair. A promenade of London plane trees has been planted and a bathhouse built. A gazebo is planned for the tip of Malibu Beach.

Savin and Malibu beaches are off Morrissey Boulevard in Dorchester. Telephone: 617-727-6034.

Lifeguards are posted daily in the summer.

By subway: Take the MBTA Red Line to the Savin Hill stop. Follow Savin Hill Avenue one quarter mile to Savin Hill and Malibu Beach

By car: From Boston, Cambridge, the north, or the south, take the Southeast Expressway (I-93) to the JFK/Columbia Road exit. Go east at the exit to the rotary and follow Morrissey Boulevard one half mile south to Malibu Beach.

Parking: There is limited free parking near the beach.

Tenean Beach, Dorchester

Tenean Beach, on a tributary near the mouth of the Neponset River, is a swimming beach with playground facilities, tennis and basketball courts. It has been resanded and newly landscaped, and a bathhouse is planned.

Tenean Beach is on Conley Road in Dorchester. Telephone: 617-727-6034.

Lifeguards are posted daily in the summer.

By subway: Take the MBTA Red Line to the Savin Hill stop. Take Bus 20 to the beach.

By car: From Boston, Cambridge, the north, or the south, take the Southeast Expressway (I-93) to the JFK/Columbia Road exit. Go east at the exit to the rotary and follow Morrissey Boulevard one half mile south past Malibu Beach to the next rotary. Make a U-turn at the rotary and exit right onto Tenean Street. Take the first left onto Conley Street, following it under I-93 to the beach.

Parking: There is limited free parking near the beach.

Carson Beach and L Street Beach, South Boston

The adjoining Carson and L Street beaches comprise the largest part of the continuous three miles of beaches and parkland along the South Boston shoreline. Always popular, both beaches saw a decline in attendance when the bathhouse complex, built in 1924, started falling into disrepair. A fire in 1996 made the situation even worse. Now the bathhouse, named for former state attorney general Edward J. McCormack, Jr., has been renovated, and outdoor showers added. A seasonal beachside café has opened, and there is an outdoor plaza with shuffleboard, bocce, and chess tables. The beach has been resanded, and there is a new boardwalk and a path from here to the John F. Kennedy Library and Museum in Dorchester, the longest single existing section of the planned 49-mile HarborWalk. New traffic signals also have been added to help pedestrians cross Day Boulevard to the beach.

Carson Beach and L Street Beach are along Day Boulevard in South Boston. Telephone: 617-727-5114.

Lifeguards are posted daily in the summer.

By subway: Take the MBTA Red Line to the UMass/JFK station and walk across Day Boulevard; or take Bus 7 from South Station or buses 9 or 11 from Broadway on the Red Line or Copley on the Green Line.

By car: From Boston, Cambridge, the north, or the south, take the Southeast Expressway (I-93) to the JFK/Columbia Road exit. Go east at the exit to the rotary, and follow the signs to Day Boulevard.

Parking: There is limited free parking along the beach.

Pleasure Bay, South Boston

The only ocean beach in Boston designed by Frederick Law Olmsted, Pleasure Bay is part of Olmsted's Marine Park and sits in a protected cove. The beach has been resanded and outdoor showers, drinking fountains, shaded shelters, and landscaping have been added.

Pleasure Bay is on Day Boulevard in South Boston. For more information telephone: 617-727-5114.

Lifeguards are posted daily in the summer.

By subway: Take the MBTA Red Line to the UMass/JFK station and

walk across Day Boulevard; or take Bus 7 from South Station or buses 9 or 11 from Broadway on the Red Line or Copley on the Green Line.

By car: From Boston, Cambridge, the north, or the south, take the Southeast Expressway (I-93) to Morrissey Boulevard. Go east at the exit to the rotary, and follow the signs to Day Boulevard.

Parking: There is limited free parking near the beach.

Constitution Beach, East Boston

This 20-acre beach and park is not exactly the city's quietest, wedged as it is between the MBTA Blue Line tracks and Logan Airport. But it has a great view of the Boston skyline. A pedestrian overpass has been built above the T tracks, opening a new gateway from Bennington Street to the park, where shaded shelters, water fountains, a playground, and a bathhouse have been built, along with outdoor showers, picnic tables, benches made out of recycled plastic, and tennis and handball courts. There is a seasonal food concession. The ethnic nature of the neighborhood is usually evident in the languages being spoken here by residents who have laid out their blankets or set up their beach chairs—predominantly but not exclusively Italian, Portuguese, and Spanish.

This beach also has an interesting neighbor. Near Bennington and Wordsworth streets next door is the state's first legally authorized Jewish cemetery. By law, Jews could not be buried in Massachusetts until 1844, when the law was changed, allowing the Temple Ohabei Shalom Cemetery to be opened here. Before that time, the deceased had to be shipped to Rhode Island, the West Indies, or even Europe. Among those buried in this cemetery: Isaac Rosnosky, the first Jewish member of the state House of Representatives.

Constitution Beach is located on Bennington Street in East Boston. Telephone: 617-727-5114.

Lifeguards are posted daily in the summer.

By subway: Take the MBTA Blue Line to Orient Heights station.

By car: From Boston, Cambridge, or the south, take the Central Artery (I-93) to the Callahan Tunnel, following the signs to Logan Airport. Go past the airport entrance to Wordsworth Street. Take a right on Wordsworth Street to Bennington Street, and a left on Bennington Street to the beach.

From the north, take Route 1A to Wordsworth Street. Take a left on Wordsworth Street to Bennington Street, and a left on Bennington Street to the beach.

Parking: There is very limited free parking near the beach.

Marine Park's Pleasure Bay offers a rolling sandy beach, tree-lined walking paths, and excellent sunbathing.

Other Notable Boston Parks

There are more than 5,000 acres of parks in Boston, nearly seven times as much area as the original Shawmut Peninsula, the spit of land that European settlers first settled on. This open park space ranges from a fraction of an acre to the newest addition, the 100-acre Millennium Park—bigger than the Boston Common and Public Garden combined—converted from a former landfill in West Roxbury in 2000. There are also 65 squares, 16 historic burying grounds, three active cemeteries, and two golf courses. Some of these parks are particularly historic, famous, scenic, innovative, and distinctive.

The Esplanade (Charles River Reservation)

The strip of grass that fronts the Boston side of the Charles River is familiar as the site of the nationally televised Boston Pops annual Fourth of July concert and fireworks display, which attracts a live audience of a half million people. Yet the Esplanade and other sections of the riverbank also boast the nation's oldest public sailing program, its largest rowing race, and other superlative places and events.

The banks of the Charles were crammed with unsightly wharves, warehouses, and slaughterhouses during most of the 19th century.

Frederick Law Olmsted wanted to incorporate a riverside park as part of the Emerald Necklace. But in 1880 the Boston Parks Commission chose instead to build a small 10-acre park near the mouth of the river as a recreational facility for low-income residents of the West End tenement neighborhood. Children in such slums received too little light and air, according to the common wisdom at the time, and needed open-air facilities. Olmsted designed a park called Charlesbank along the river between Cambridge Street and Leverett Street, with separate open-air gymnasiums for men and women, a railed promenade along the water, and for children some of the first sandboxes in America. These gymnasiums were the first of their kind in the country operated free of charge in a public park, with equipment including horizontal bars and trapezes. Doctors began recommending to their patients that they spend time there; within a few years, average daily attendance in the women's gymnasium alone—administered by the Massachusetts Emergency and Hygiene Association—was 840 in the summer.

Olmsted's disciple Charles Eliot, meanwhile, pushed for the development of the entire Charles River basin, beginning at the West End but continuing nine miles upstream on both sides. It would be the "central

A sphinxlike rendition of the late conductor Arthur Fiedler gazes fondly at the Charles Bank Esplanade where he first led the Boston Pops Orchestra in 1929. Below, blossoming cherry trees offer a sensory delight to an inline skater traversing a part of the 17-mile long Charles River pathway.

court of honor in the metropolitan district," Eliot said. This gave way to the idea of the Metropolitan Park Commission—now the Metropolitan District Commission—and by 1895 about 17 miles of riverbanks were publicly owned.

Even then, much of the river was a saltwater mudflat when the tide went out. The river's mouth was dammed in 1910, stabilizing the water level and allowing work on the parks to proceed. The campaign to build the dam had been led by a wealthy banker named James Jackson Storrow, and when Storrow died in 1930, his widow, Helen, gave $1 million to create a park along the Esplanade on the condition that a road never be built there. Landscape architect Arthur Shurcliff, another Olmsted student, laid out lagoons and paths and the Music Oval, where a bandstand was placed in the summer. Conductor Arthur Fiedler and the Boston Pops moved their

Independence Day performances there until, in 1941, a permanent stage was built: the Edward Hatch Memorial Shell. Meanwhile, in 1936, school committee member Joseph Lee, Jr., had founded a public sailing program called Community Boating to keep the children of the West End off the streets when school was not in session. In 1941 it moved to a new boathouse paid for by Helen Storrow, just behind the new Hatch Shell.

For all of this activity, the park was suddenly and definitively severed from the city's residential neighborhoods beginning in 1949, when, after Helen Storrow died, the state legislature decided to build a road between the two. They added insult to injury by naming it Storrow Drive, even though it violated the terms of her bequest. To make up for the land lost to the road, more of the river was filled in to enlarge the Esplanade—and Olmsted's Charlesbank. Though Charlesbank was

Boston's famous Hatch Memorial Shell on the Esplanade at the Charles River serves as the stage for the Boston Pops Orchestra and its famous Fourth of July concert. Watched on television by some 500,000 people it includes an obligatory rendition of Tchaikovsky's "1812 Overture" followed by a spectacular firework exhibition.

obliterated by the road construction project, it was replaced by an MDC swimming pool and an athletic field near the same site.

Today the Esplanade and its adjoining parks also boast an 18-mile bicycle path. The art deco–style Hatch Shell, newly renovated, has an inlaid interior pattern of wood and the names of the world's foremost composers along its edge, from Bach to Gershwin. In addition to the Pops concerts, there is jazz, dance, contemporary music, and free Friday night movies while the shell is open between June and October. Community Boating also continues to offer $1 sailboat rentals for children. Besides the Fourth of July extravaganza, the river's biggest party is the annual Head of the Charles regatta, held the third weekend of October, the largest rowing race in the world.

There are monuments and sculptures all around the river, most notably four near the Hatch Shell. The first is a larger-than-life bronze of General George S. Patton, Jr., standing in uniform and holding a pair of binoculars, just west of the Longfellow Bridge. It's a copy of a statue at the U.S. Military Academy at West Point by sculptor James Earle Fraser, and it's here because Patton was married to the daughter of a wealthy Boston textile manufacturer. A Civil War hero, Major General Charles Devens, is also memorialized near the Hatch Shell; it was for him that Fort Devens in Ayer was named. There also is a life-size bronze near the Hatch Shell of Maurice J. Tobin, mayor from 1938 until 1944, governor in 1946 and 1947, and U.S. Secretary of Labor beginning in 1949 under President Harry Truman. But the most unusual work is the massive bust of the beloved Arthur Fiedler, carved from layers of aluminum of various thicknesses by Cambridge sculptor Ralph Helmick.

The Charles River Esplanade is open daily from dawn until 11 p.m. The Esplanade runs along Storrow Drive between Cambridge Street and Massachusetts Avenue. Telephone: 617-635-4505.

How to Get to the Esplanade

By subway: Take the MBTA Red Line to Charles Street or take the Green Line to Science Park or the Green Line to Arlington Street. Walk north on Arlington Street to the Arthur Fiedler footbridge and cross Storrow Drive into the park.

By car: From Cambridge, cross the Charles River at Massachusetts Avenue to the Esplanade side.

From the west, take the Massachusetts Turnpike (I-90) to the Copley Square exit. At the end of the exit, go two blocks to Berkeley Street and take a left on Berkeley to Beacon Street.

From the south, take the Southeast Expressway (I-93) to the Massachusetts Avenue exit. Take a right at the end of the exit and follow Massachusetts Avenue to Commonwealth Avenue. Take a right on Commonwealth, and the first left to Beacon Street.

Parking: There is no parking at the Esplanade. Limited metered parking is available on Beacon Street.

Christopher Columbus Park

During much of the 20th century, Boston turned its back on the waterfront where it began, building an elevated highway that divided the city from the harbor, and allowing construction all along the shore. It was not until 1976 that this four-and-a-half-acre park was built, connecting the Quincy Market area with the rejuvenated Boston Harbor docks and opening up a vista to the water. It was named Christopher Columbus Park, and a statue of the famous

Christopher Columbus Park is a perfect spot for a picnic, and not far from Fanueil Hall where you can pick up sandwiches to go. The area also boasts a beautiful rose garden dedicated to Rose Fitzgerald Kennedy, who was born nearby.

explorer by sculptor Andrew Mazzola stands as its centerpiece. Widely disliked, the statue is a favorite target of impish vandals who like to rouge its lips. More distinctive is the 340-foot-long arched trellis covered with leafy vines, where visitors can sit and look out at the harbor (and the decidedly unappealing view of Logan International Airport) and a small rose garden dedicated to Rose Fitzgerald Kennedy, who was born nearby at 4 Garden Court in the North End.

Christopher Columbus Park is open from 6 a.m. until 11:30 p.m., though foot traffic continues at all hours.

The park is on Atlantic Avenue between Long and Commercial wharves.

How to Get to Columbus Park

By subway: Take the MBTA Blue Line to Aquarium.

By car: From Cambridge, take Memorial Drive to the Longfellow Bridge over the Charles River. At the end of the bridge, go straight onto Cambridge Street. Take a left onto Sudbury Street and a right onto Atlantic Avenue. The park is on the left.

From the west, take the Massachusetts Turnpike (I-90) to the Central Artery (I-93) northbound. Take the Atlantic Avenue/Northern Avenue exit, and follow Atlantic Avenue to the park.

From the north, take I-93 south-bound to the airport exit. At the end of the exit, continue straight onto Atlantic Avenue. The park is on the left.

From the south, take the Southeast Expressway (I-93) to the Central Artery. Take the Atlantic Avenue/Northern Avenue exit, and follow Atlantic Avenue to the park.

Parking: There is no parking at this park. Parking is available at several local parking garages.

Post Office Square

A jewel in the packed Financial District, Post Office Square serves as an urban refuge for office workers who descend upon it every autumn, spring, and summer day at lunchtime. Their gratitude for this small (1.7-acre) space is understandable, considering its history—and considering that another sparse commodity, parking for 1,400 cars, is hidden underneath it.

There once stood on this space an ugly, three-level above-ground concrete parking garage that marred the view from the surrounding buildings and threw shadows that darkened the street. By the 1980s, when real estate prices in downtown Boston hit their peak, 20 surrounding businesses contributed $1 million each toward the ultimate $80 million cost of tearing down the concrete structure and replacing it with a park whose costs were to be underwritten with the profits of a new

A treasured park, especially loved by area workers at lunchtime, sits atop an enormous underground garage at Post Office Square. Left, vines climb along a 143-foot-long trellised colonnade in a park with 125 species of plants and six large trees from the Arnold Arboretum. Above, Howard Ben Tré's bronze-and-green-glass fountain sculpture on the north plaza.

garage underground. The rest of the money was raised by selling stock; all 450 preferred shares were sold in just six weeks.

At a cost of about $34,000 per space, the garage was one of the most expensive ever built; *The Wall Street Journal*, whose Boston bureau is across the street, called it the "Garage Mahal." It required the deepest excavation in Boston history, 80 feet, to accommodate its seven levels of parking. There is also a lavish underground lobby with polished granite walls, a car wash, and an automated checkout system. It took five years to negotiate the complicated construction deal and four more to build the project.

The garage generates about $8 million a year to cover its debt service, taxes, and the operating costs of the above-ground park, which is privately guarded and maintained, and looks it. The site is kept pristine, and there is free live music at lunchtime in the summer. The park and garage design have won more than 20 planning and architectural awards. Once the debt is paid off, the city will receive all the profits from the garage. The money will be allocated to other neighborhood parks.

At the oldest, pointed end of the square is the site of the first post office in America, which opened here in 1639. Now called Angell Memorial Plaza, it is dominated by a huge memorial to George Thorndike Angell, who founded the Massachusetts Society for the Protection of Animals in 1868 after watching two horses raced to death. Angell also founded the American Humane Society. The memorial consists of a high stone column with four brass lions at its foot and a gold eagle at its peak. Beside it is a newer sculpture, called the Creature Pond: a bronze pond in a circular stone base 14 feet in diameter with sculpted lily pads, frogs, ducks, turtles, even a lizard on a rock. It was a collaboration of nine artists in 1982.

The modern park begins across Milk Street. Here the fernlike bright green leaves of Halka honey locusts shade benches that follow the contours of a raised curb. In the middle is a ring of thick cubes of aqua-colored frosted, or "cast," glass, atop five 11-foot bronze-on-granite pillars. Water shoots in narrow jets from the ring and from a circle at its base. Installed in 1992, the fountain is the work of sculptor Howard Ben Tré. Beyond this the paths diverge around a grassy median. On the left is a 143-foot corridor covered by a trellis draped with tiny lights. It leads to the glass-and-steel pedestrian exit from the garage, which is designed to look like a greenhouse. Another building in the same style, to the right, houses a popular snack bar.

Tucked away off the lobby of an office building across the street at this end, incidentally, is the room where one of the most important technological advancements in the modern era came about: the laboratory where Alexander Graham Bell invented the telephone. Bell's lab was where the Boston University professor and determined inventor sent the first coherent spoken message—"Come here, Watson, I want you!"—on March 10, 1876. Originally at 109 Court Street (where a plaque near the John F. Kennedy Federal Building marks the site), the lab was disassembled when that building was torn down in 1959. It was reassembled in the headquarters of what was then the New England Telephone and Telegraph Company, now the Verizon building. The first telephone patent, which was granted March 7, 1876, is on display here. The window is original, as are the timbers, rafters, sheathing and floorboards, all authenticated by Bell's assistant, Thomas A. Watson, himself. Also on exhibit: the world's first commercial telephone, and the first telephone switchboard, installed at 342 Washington Street on May 17, 1877.

Post Office Square and the Post Office Square garage are open 24 hours. From mid-May until September, concerts are held in the park on Tuesdays and Thursdays between 12:15 p.m. and 1:45 p.m. The Bell lab in the Verizon building is open Monday through Friday, 9 a.m. to 5 p.m. Admission is free.

The park is bordered by Milk, Pearl, Congress, and Franklin streets. Telephone: 617-423-1500. The Verizon building is at 185 Franklin Street.

How to Get to Post Office Square

By subway: Take the MBTA Orange Line to Downtown Crossing, the Blue or Orange lines to State Street, or the Green or Red lines to Park Street.

By car: From Cambridge, take Memorial Drive to the Longfellow Bridge over the Charles River. At the end of the bridge, go straight on Cambridge Street, then right on Congress, which runs directly to the park.

From the west, take the Massachusetts Turnpike (I-90) to the Central Artery (I-93) northbound. Take the Atlantic Avenue/ Northern Avenue exit. Take a left on High Street and a right on Pearl Street.

From the south, take the Southeast Expressway (I-93) to the Atlantic Avenue/Northern Avenue exit. Take a left on High Street and a right on Pearl Street.

Parking: Parking is available

underneath the park in the Post Office Square Garage.

Copley Square

One of the preeminent cityscapes in this most picturesque of cities, Copley Square is dominated by Trinity Church, rated by the American Institute of Architects as one of the 10 finest public buildings in America. Set aside during the filling of the Back Bay for civic and religious buildings, the square today ranges from the somber backdrop of the Anglican church to the mischievous sculpture of a turtle and a hare devoted to the Boston Marathon. There also are concerts, a busy farmers market on Tuesdays and Fridays, and a half-price ticket booth.

Trinity Church was designed by Frederick Law Olmsted's Brookline neighbor H. H. Richardson in the French Romanesque style. The murals inside were the work of John La Farge, who was known for not only his murals, but his oils, watercolors, stained-glass windows, and book and magazine illustrations. The Trinity murals were the first major public decorative project in America executed by a painter.

To the left of the church is a larger-than-life bronze of Phillips Brooks, its larger-than-life rector. Brooks weighed 300 pounds and is

Copley Square has been a focus for Boston architecture since the 19th century. With Trinity Church, center, H. H. Richardson reached the peak of his career and created one of the great monuments of American architecture.

best known as the author of "O Little Town of Bethlehem." The statue portrays Jesus laying his hand on the shoulder of Brooks at prayer. It is by Augustus Saint-Gaudens, who also created the 54th Regiment Memorial on Boston Common, but it was finished by his students as he lay terminally ill. Less solemn are the tortoise and the hare, commemorating the 100th anniversary of the famous marathon that ends a block from here. They are the work of Nancy Schön, who also crafted the ducklings statue in the Public Garden. A map of the marathon route is inlaid in the plaza on the Boylston Street side. In between is a decorative fountain that is a popular lunchtime respite for the workers in this neighborhood.

Many of those workers have their offices in the 60-story John Hancock Tower, the tallest building north of New York, designed by I.M. Pei. When the tower was completed in 1975, its weight pressed down into the spongy landfill, and Trinity Church began to sink. The developers sank pilings to stabilize the square, and now the church is strikingly reflected in the blue glass of the adjoining high-rise.

Next among the buildings surrounding the square is the Fairmont Copley Plaza Hotel, built in 1912 and designed by the architect Clarence Blackall, who also devised the Colonial Theatre and the Winthrop Building on Washington Street, the first steel-frame structure in Boston. There's another piece of marathon memorabilia in the lobby: the bronzed running shoes of Johnny Kelley, who competed in the Boston Marathon 61 times, won it twice, and came in second seven times. The Museum of Fine Arts originally was on this site before moving to its current home on Huntington Avenue.

Opposite the church is the Boston Public Library, the first free municipal library in America supported by general taxation. Completed in 1899, the Beaux Arts–style classic was designed by the architectural firm McKim, Meade & White. The addition to the rear was built in 1972, the work of architect Philip Johnson, whose other buildings include Boston's International Place.

The library houses a largely unknown collection of art on free public display, including more works by Augustus and Louis Saint-

Gaudens, Daniel Chester French, John Singleton Copley, Winslow Homer, James Abbott McNeill Whistler, John James Audubon, Rembrandt, Goya, Picasso, Toulouse-Lautrec, Rockwell Kent, and Alfred Stieglitz. There are also murals, on the third floor of the McKim Building: John Singer Sargent's *Judaism and Christianity*, showing the development of world religions, which he considered his greatest achievement; and *The Quest of the Holy Grail*, by Edwin Austin Abbey, with 150 life-sized figures illustrating the legends of King Arthur. In its research room, the library exhibits some of its rare-book holdings, which include Shakespeare first folios and the personal papers of President John Adams.

Copley Square is open from 6 a.m. until 11:30 p.m., though foot traffic continues at all hours. The Boston Public Library is open Monday through Thursday 9 a.m. to 9 p.m., Friday and Saturday 9 a.m. to 5 p.m., Sunday 1 p.m. to 5 p.m., and closed Sunday June through September.

The square is bounded by Boylston, Clarendon, Dartmouth, and St. James streets. There is a library entrance on the square and a second entrance at 700 Boylston Street.

How to Get to Copley Square

By car: From Cambridge, take Memorial Drive to the Longfellow Bridge over the Charles River. At the end of the bridge, take a right onto Charles Street. Take a right on Beacon Street and a left on Clarendon Street to Copley Square.

From the west, take the Massachusetts Turnpike (I-90) to the Copley Square exit.

From the south or north, take Interstate 93 to the Massachusetts Avenue exit. Take a right at the end of the exit and follow Massachusetts Avenue to Boylston Street. Go right onto Boylston Street, which runs directly to the square.

Parking: There is limited metered parking on Boylston Street and off-street parking under the Prudential Center just to the west of the Boston Public Library, with entrances on Boylston Street and Huntington Avenue; and in the Copley Place office, hotel, and shopping complex, with an entrance on Huntington Avenue.

Marine Park (Castle Island)

One of Boston's most pleasant waterfront parks also is in one of its most important settings: Marine Park, which encompasses historic Castle Island in South Boston. Castle isn't actually an island any more, having been connected to the mainland by a causeway in the 1930s. But it is the oldest continually fortified site in what was British North America. There has been some kind of defensive structure here since the Puritans built an earthworks with three cannon in 1634. That was replaced by a fort made partially of wood, which burned down in 1674; then by a new brick-and-stone fort named Fort William after King William IV. It was here that the British had their headquarters during the siege of Boston at the outset of the Revolutionary War—until, in one of the most pivotal (and largely forgotten) moments in American history, George Washington secretly emplaced 59 cannon on Dorchester

In 1634, the first fortification on Castle Island was an earthworks with three cannon. The present granite structure, Fort Independence, is the eighth fort to occupy this site and was constructed between 1834 and 1851.

Heights under cover of darkness on the night of March 4, 1776. The cannon had been dragged 300 miles by oxen from Fort Ticonderoga. When the British awoke to find the guns pointing directly down at them, they fled. (This event is commemorated by a 215-foot marble monument on Dorchester Heights, and a city holiday, Evacuation Day, conveniently held to coincide with St. Patrick's Day each March 17.) It was Washington's first major victory. Before they left, of course, the British burned the fort; but it was rebuilt in 1778, and in 1799 was rededicated by President John Adams as Fort Independence.

Like many of the harbor islands, Castle also has a literary history. The friends of a Lieutenant Robert Massie, who was shot dead in a Christmas Day duel over a card game in 1817, sealed his killer alive in a chamber deep in the dungeons of the fort. A sullen private named Edgar Allen Poe, posted to Fort Independence 10 years later, heard about the incident and used it as the basis for his story, "The Cask of Amontillado." In 1905, workers repairing an abandoned casement found a skeleton in military uniform sealed in the wall. The man was never identified.

The current incarnation of the fort was completed in 1851 after 17 years of work. It was used as a harbor defense during the Civil War. Like every other fort ever built there, it was informally called the Castle, giving the 22-acre island its name.

Olmsted and the Castle

Enter Frederick Law Olmsted and the Boston Parks Commission. One of the commission's first orders of business in 1876 was to call for a park near the site of the fort, the area then (and still, by most of its neighbors) known as City Point. It was to be the terminus of the Emerald Necklace, connected to Franklin Park by a series of parks and parkways that were never built. Olmsted wanted to connect the island to the mainland with a causeway, creating a round protected bay with tree-lined walkways leading to a long wooden pleasure pier that would form the far end of the oval. The walkways would sweep onto Castle Island and around the pentagonal fort. But Castle Island and Fort

From the moment it opened in 1891, Marine Park—or Pleasure Bay as Olmsted had originally named it—became a popular attraction. Here, a year later, visitors promenade on the temporary pier.

Independence were federal property. It literally required an act of Congress for the plan to be approved, a process that took 14 years. Marine Park finally opened in 1891. The locals immediately dubbed it the Bowl.

Instead of a causeway, Castle Island was connected to the mainland with a footbridge. The pier proved extremely popular, and there was a bathhouse and boathouses. But the military took back the island and closed it off to public access during the Spanish-American War, and again during World War I. Olmsted's connecting causeway finally was built in 1932, but the military shut the gates a third time during World War II. The bathhouse was destroyed by a fire in 1942, and an aquarium that had been built here was torn down in the 1950s. Finally, Castle Island was handed over to the state in 1962. But while the beach remained popular, the park became neglected.

Now restored, Marine Park has its original, renovated bandstand plus a concession stand, a skating rink, a boat landing, two baseball diamonds, and a playground. It also has great views of the harbor islands to the east, the city skyline to the north, and the line of marinas known as Yacht Club Row to the south. The beach has been replen-

ished, there are seasonal swimming and sailing lessons, and the steep glacial drumlins near the skating rink are popular for sledding. Walkers and bicyclists flock to Castle Island on the weekends to explore Fort Independence, now on the National Historic Register of Places, or to watch the planes taking off from Logan International Airport just across the harbor.

Two monuments also stand inside the park. One, on Castle Island, is of Donald McKay of East Boston, father of the clipper ship, who built some of the fastest and sleekest sailing vessels of the first half of the 19th century. Among them: the famous *Flying Cloud*, which broke the established record for a voyage around Cape Horn. The other is a statue of Admiral David Farragut by the sculptor Henry Hudson Kitson, whose other works include the Minuteman statue on Lexington Common. Farragut was a Tennessee-born Union Navy hero of the Civil War who led the blockade of the South and was famous for saying: "Damn the torpedoes! Full speed ahead." The statue, completed in 1883, is at the entrance to the park near the intersection of Day Boulevard and Broadway.

Marine Park and Castle Island are open daily from 8 a.m. to dusk. The Dorchester Heights Monument is open Saturday and Sunday from 10 a.m. to 4 p.m. and Wednesday 4 p.m. to 8 p.m. between Memorial Day and Labor Day.

Marine Park is at the end of Day

Roxbury High Fort was built when the siege was at its peak, on high ground that protected the approach to Roxbury. Abandoned the next year when the threat evaporated, the earthworks nonetheless remained visible until well into the 19th century, when they were leveled to accommodate a tall, thin water tower called a standpipe in 1869. The standpipe was built to look like a Bavarian turret. Though it was made obsolete when a new reservoir was built nearby in 1880, it remained standing and became an observation tower and the centerpiece of the little park built beginning in 1888.

Frederick Law Olmsted's firm got the commission to develop Fort Hill. In addition to retaining the standpipe, its design called for reconstructing the Revolutionary War–era earthworks and adding landscaping and low walls made out of Roxbury puddingstone.

Highland Park is open from 6 a.m. until 11:30 p.m.

The park is at Fulda and Highland streets in Boston's Roxbury section.

Boulevard in South Boston. The Dorchester Heights Monument is at 456 West 4th Street, South Boston. For information about the monument, call 617-242-5642.

How to Get to Marine Park

By subway: Take the MBTA Red Line to the UMass/JFK station and follow Day Boulevard to the park; or take Bus 7 from South Station or buses 9 or 11 from Broadway on the Red Line or Copley on the Green Line.

By car: From Boston, Cambridge, the north, or the south, take the Southeast Expressway (I-93) to Morrissey Boulevard. Go east at the exit to the rotary, and follow the signs to Day Boulevard.

Parking: Limited parking is available at the park.

Fort Hill

A lot of history is packed onto tiny Fort Hill. Even if it wasn't, the view of downtown Boston from Highland Park at the top is unequaled. You can find it by what looks like the turret of a Bavarian castle, a surreal landmark towering over Roxbury.

The tower stands on the site of Roxbury High Fort, built by Henry Knox in June 1775 to help end the British occupation of Boston. Knox would later be the man who transported those cannon from Fort Ticonderoga to Dorchester Heights to rout the British in the siege of Boston. In 1783, he succeeded Washington as commander of the army, and was the first U.S. Secretary of War.

How to Get to Fort Hill

By subway: Take the MBTA Orange Line to Jackson Square. Take a right at the exit from the station, and a left on Columbus Avenue. Walk to Cedar Street. Take a right onto Cedar Street and an immediate right onto Fort Avenue and look for the Bavarian turret.

By car: From Cambridge, the north, or the south, take the Southeast Expressway (I-93), to the Massachusetts Avenue exit. At the end of the exit, go straight onto Melnea Cass Boulevard. Take Melnea Cass to Tremont Street. Go left on Tremont, which becomes Columbus Avenue. Take a left on Cedar Street and an immediate right on Fort Avenue, and look for the Bavarian turret.

From the west, take the Massachusetts Turnpike (I-90) to take the Southeast Expressway (I-93) southbound, to the Massachusetts Avenue exit. At the end of the exit, go straight onto Melnea Cass Boulevard. Take Melnea Cass to Tremont Street. Go left on Tremont, which becomes Columbus Avenue. Take a left on Cedar Street and an immediate right on Fort Avenue, and look for the Bavarian turret.

Parking: There is limited parking on the streets around the park.

The Frederick Law Olmsted National Historic Site

Frederick Law Olmsted was 60 when he bought his first permanent home in Brookline, a five-minute walk from the Muddy River parks he had designed as part of Boston's Emerald Necklace.

The estate he crafted from an antique farmhouse on a scant 2 acres of land—which he could not resist sublimely naming Fairsted—would incorporate many of his design ideas in that small space, including rough-hewn stone steps and sloping lawns. Its tiny rock garden is reminiscent of Central Park's Ramble. Its sunken grotto, called the Hollow, inspired the Ravine Garden at the Indianapolis Museum of Fine Art and the Quarry Garden at Stan Hywet Hall, on the estate of Goodyear Tire and Rubber cofounder F. A. Seiberling in Akron, Ohio. All were designed by Olmsted students and disciples.

Fairsted was not only Olmsted's studio and office; it was effectively the only school of landscape design in America from its inception in 1884 until Olmsted's son, Frederick Law Olmsted, Jr., established the first formal training program in landscape architecture at Harvard in 1900; Charles Eliot, Warren Manning, Henry Sargent Codman, Arthur Shurcliff, James Frederick Dawson, and Henry Vincent Hubbard all worked here as young men before going on to prestigious careers in the emergent field. And for the first half of the 20th century, Fairsted housed the largest and most important landscape architecture practice in the nation.

Olmsted's Home and Office

Olmsted had always been fond of Brookline, which he visited for three successive summers in the early 1880s, and where friends including Arnold Arboretum director Charles Sprague Sargent and architect H. H. Richardson already lived. A good city needed a good suburb, Olmsted liked to say, and Brookline's winding streets and rural nature appealed to both his personal and professional side. Long an agricultural town, it had become popular with Boston's rich, who built huge summer homes and "gentlemen's farms" of 100 acres and more there. The effect of this was to preserve the town's agricultural character, while also making it

Frederick Law Olmsted in 1893

sufficiently civilized and intellectual for Olmsted.

In the summer of 1881, Olmsted stayed with friends on Brookline's Cottage Street. He already had his eye on what would become Fairsted, but the sisters who owned the place wouldn't sell. Property rich but cash poor, they rented rooms and used the land to harvest orchard fruits, firewood, and summer grass for cattle. In 1882, Olmsted summered in the same neighborhood, in a house near the Walnut Street Cemetery. Still, the sisters wouldn't budge. In 1883, he rented the Taylor Estate,

also near the Fairsted site. The sisters hadn't changed their minds. Exasperated, Olmsted's stepson, John Charles Olmsted, by then a partner in his father's firm, offered to build the women a new house on the property. Finally, they agreed to go.

Olmsted the elder moved in with his wife of 24 years, Mary, and three of their seven children: John Charles, who was 31; Frederick Jr., who was 13; and Marion, who was 22, who would live there all her life. The house needed work, and Olmsted quickly got to it. Nearly 200 varieties of trees, shrubs, and ground cover were planted on the grounds, and the parlor was extended by 10 feet to accommodate an office with desks, walls of bookshelves, and a long drafting table in the center where plans could be unrolled and read. The business would take up the north and east sides of the house, the residential quarters the south and west. Shutters and vines were installed to insulate the windows from the summer heat. Olmsted held that the contemplation of quiet pastoral scenery was therapeutic, and relaxing views were crafted outside every window. But inside, five men shared the drafting room, and things were getting crowded.

The Olmsteds started to add a

A magnificent American elm towers over the house. There are more than 30 species of trees on the grounds, including a massive Canadian hemlock that Olmsted planted when he first came to Fairsted.

wing of offices stretching out toward Dudley Street. They would continue adding on for 40 years as the firm grew. When they neared the edge of the property, they started building vertically, attaching a second story. In 1930, the firm accommodated 69 employees here.

Olmsted senior retired in 1895 and died in 1903. John Charles became the senior partner of the firm until his death at 68 in 1920. A savvy businessman largely credited with keeping new commissions coming in from all over the country, he was the first president of the American Society of Landscape Architects in 1899, and himself laid out the campuses of Smith College and the University of Chicago, and the Seattle park system. Frederick Law Olmsted, Jr., studied at Harvard and apprenticed on projects including the 1893 World's Columbian Exposition in Chicago and the Biltmore Estate in North Carolina. He took over as senior partner when his brother died, and inherited Fairsted when Mary Olmsted died at

91 in 1921. Rather than live there himself, he rented out the residential quarters. Frederick Law Olmsted, Jr., designed the White House carriage roads, Acadia National Park in Maine, Palos Verdes Estates in California, Rock Creek Park in Washington, D.C., and Fort Tryon Park in New York. He retired in 1949, and died at 87 in 1957.

By then, the Olmsted firm was in decline. The National Park Service acquired the property, and opened it as a National Historic Site in 1981, beginning a long process of restoration. What the government wanted most was the firm's estimated one million documents—including topographic studies, 150,000 landscape architecture plans and 70,000 photographs of 5,000 important parks, estates, campuses, and grounds.

Today, the Olmsted Archives is one of the most comprehensive and widely-researched collections in the National Park Service. These documents are critical to the research, rehabilitation, and protection of public and private Olmsted-designed landscapes nationwide.

His home, the elder Olmsted once said, was meant to be "a quiescent and cheerfully musing state of mind" where "the eye is not drawn to dwell upon nor the mind to be occupied with details."

At Fairsted, it turns out, the details are the most interesting parts.

 ## A Walking Tour of Fairsted

Fairsted's entrance from Warren Street is by way of a decorative spruce-pole arch that evokes the shape of a thatched-roof cottage, framing a circular carriage turn. In the center of this driveway is a massive Canadian hemlock tree, which Olmsted planted almost as soon as he moved in—at which time he said it wouldn't look as he wanted it until at least 100 years had passed. Today its trunk is hung with ivy and its countless branches form a latticework so thick that it's hard to make out the house. That's a conscious part of the design. The house is sprawling, but it has been made subordinate to the surrounding landscape with a color scheme of dark green trim and shutters, and walls the red of maple leaves in autumn. Olmsted counseled that a structure painted white could not blend in with nature; some of the newer, lighter-colored houses in this neighborhood prove his point.

To the right of the carriage turn is arguably Fairsted's most distinctive feature: the Hollow, a tiny sunken grotto. One side of the grotto is walled off by a vertical cliff of Roxbury puddingstone overhung with creeper vines. At the base of this wall sprawls rock cotoneaster, low spreading shrubs with semievergreen foliage that grow about three feet high. A nondescript green dur-

closest to the office entrance of the house, distinctive for its bark so deeply textured that it looks like it's about to fall off.

Across the entryway again, and just inside the arch and to the left, is a massive cucumber magnolia that was given to Olmsted by Charles Sprague Sargent. The tree produces fruits that look like red cucumbers. Just behind it is a Russian olive tree, whose fuzzy leaves look gray, and which Olmsted also used abundantly at Biltmore, the North Carolina estate he designed for George Vanderbilt. A spruce-pole fence and wild-seeming plantings—including Virginia creeper and English ivy—screen out Warren Street.

A tiny rock garden connects the south and east exposures of the property, complete with a narrow path so effectively curtained off by dogwood, mountain laurel, mock orange, viburnum, and a tapestry of ferns that employees labeled it the "secret room." Modern-day park rangers joke that the tiny path through the rock garden is the shortest hiking trail in the National Park Service.

The little trail quickly reemerges on the South Lawn, whose irregular shape and sloping surface bordered by an undulating wave of shrubs makes it appear considerably bigger than it actually is—a common Olmsted trick. A single giant elm

ing most of the year, they turn red in the fall and develop colorful red fruit in the winter. There are also rhododendron and azalea bushes.

A trademark Olmsted stone stairway descends to the floor of the grotto, and a short irregular path leads across it to what was once the employee lunchroom (for men only; the women secretaries ate separately). In the center are wild irises with a backdrop of hay-scented fern that grows as fragrant in the summer as the Hollow is colorful in the fall. A flowering dogwood overhangs the scene, and there's an aptly named shagbark hickory in the grotto

The tiny rock garden connecting the south and east exposures of the property has a narrow path that park rangers joke is the shortest hiking trail in the National Park Service.

towers over the lawn and screens the home's conservatory, which Olmsted called his out-of-doors apartment, from which he could view almost the entire property. The South Lawn is a miniature Olmsted landscape.

Inside the House

Through the entrance of the house and to the right is the administrative wing and the beginning of the Olmsteds' patchwork of additions; to the immediate left is that original main drafting room, which was created by extending the parlor of the farmhouse by 10 feet in 1884. The bookcases and the desks are gone, but the table in the center of the room is reminiscent of Olmsted's long drafting table. Five men competed with all that furniture in Olmsted's time. The walls were hung with framed reproductions of his notable works, including New York's Central Park and the U.S. Capitol grounds, and a fire blazed in the fireplace all winter.

"His office always looked like what it was," Frederick Law Olmsted, Jr., said of his father's workspace, "part of his home comfortably adapted to office use." Today, a large photograph of Prospect Park in Brooklyn hangs above the mantelpiece, and on the walls are pictures of the men who worked here, often in playful poses that belie their later prominence as the first of the new professional class of landscape architects. In one, Arthur Shurcliff can be seen clowning around by hanging from a gutter. Shurcliff would go on to design the grounds of Colonial Williamsburg.

Touring Upstairs

The Olmsteds began expanding the business wing of Fairsted piece by piece. The ultimate footprint was complete by 1904, though the expansion would continue after that time with the addition of a second story. Since the estate has been restored to the way it looked in 1930, around the height of the firm's commercial success, our tour will focus on this upper level. The lower level houses Park Service staff, and the residential section of the house is used for exhibits and visitor orientation. (It doesn't look the way it did when Olmsted lived there anyway, as

John Charles Olmsted, left, checking a drawing at his worktable. The offices, with their 1930s furnishings and reproductions of plans, drawings, and photographs can be seen by visitors to the site.

Frederick Law Olmsted, Jr., rented it out to boarders after his mother died in 1921.)

Through the entrance to the administrative wing and up the stairs is the wood-paneled room where the firm maintained its library of photographs in endless rows of built-in wooden file drawers. Many of these photographs were cleverly arranged before-and-after fashion so a customer could see the designers' conception of what his property would look like when the Olmsteds finished with it. Others were arranged in albums, and one is on a table under the plan of the project whose design it chronicles: Rock Creek Park in Washington, D.C.

The firm used a unique numerical classification system; Boston's parks are filed under the 900s, for example. Number 9199 is the Depression-era job of landscaping a certain oceanfront estate in Hyannisport for a fellow Brookline family named Kennedy. There's an antique typewriter at the other end of the room, which could move on tracks to label the wide pages of the photo albums.

Primitive Duplicates

The next room is where the engineers sat. On the drafting table is a wooden box of plans and the blueprints of a bridge on the Jamaicaway. Engineers and draftsmen sat on backless stools and leaned on tables braced by wooden sawhorses. The considerable difficulty of duplicating design plans in the 19th century is evident in a glass-topped table with a light below it, where a junior engineer or intern traced the plans by hand, one after another.

Next is the huge upstairs drafting room, which ultimately replaced Olmsted's original expanded parlor. A telephone once hung in the connecting vestibule, which still bears the artistic doodles made by draftsmen while they were speaking on the phone; the house is filled with drawings and cartoons they made. Original knob-and-pipe wiring and gooseneck lights hang from the ceiling, whose unusual washboard-style ridged wood paneling was chosen less for its aesthetics than its safety. It's a dense flame- and insect-retardant cypress. Outside the window of this room is Olmsted's Hollow, with its flowering dogwood in the front.

The next room was devoted entirely to duplicating blueprints. The Olmsteds moved from manually tracing these designs to copying them somewhat in the manner that a photograph is made.

This, too, was crude, however. A plan was drawn on opaque paper, which was pressed against another page of equal size, treated with a combination of unpleasant chemicals, pushed through the window onto a rack outside, and exposed to the sun. This could not be done at night or when the skies were overcast, so a shower stall–size glass column was installed indoors against which the plans and drawings could be pressed while an arc light moved from top to bottom.

In the next room, the blueprints would be washed down to remove the chemicals; the raised slatted floor testifies to the mess this made. Still wet, the paper would be hung on drying frames and rolled into a heated alcove.

Next across the creaking wooden floor in the progression of these warrenlike rooms was the planting department, where trees, plants, and shrubs were chosen for a project. The planting plan on view here is for Vanderbilt's Biltmore.

A staircase ingeniously lit by a skylight (but with no handrail at the top, making it inadvisable to look around too much while descending) leads back down to the offices as they existed in the elder Olmsted's era, until the second floor was built in 1912. The first room is another drafting and mailing chamber, outside of which stands a windowless two-story brick appendage to this wooden house, which looks like a modern addition. In fact, it is the vault built by the Olmsted brothers, where each night designers were required to deposit all their plans behind thick double doors built by the Mosler bank-safe manufacturers to protect them, not from theft but from fire. The vault is beside the workers' entrance; engineers and draftsmen would begin and end their days there, claiming and depositing their plans and drawings.

Through protective glass installed by the Park Service is the extraordinary sight of original plans spilling out of their cramped shelves. It's just for show; beyond them, thousands of designs have been catalogued and stored in neat banks of drawers and tubes. But the ink bottles, telegram forms, and soapstone sink are all original. (Nor is the parking lot beyond this door a modern addition; it was built by the Olmsteds in 1926, replacing a garden.)

When the National Park Service acquired Fairsted, the contents included nearly one million documents. Many drawings and blueprints were stored casually in the vault, pictured here, without concern for their longevity. Today, they are maintained under temperature- and humidity-controlled conditions.

To complete your tour, return to the exhibit area of the house, where there is a scale model in three dimensions of the project Olmsted senior completed just as he prepared to retire from the practice in this house: Boston's Emerald Necklace.

The Frederick Law Olmsted National Historic Site is open Friday through Sunday from 10 a.m. to 4 p.m.

The site is at 99 Warren Street. Telephone: 617-566-1689.

How to Get to Fairsted

By subway: Take the MBTA Green Line to Brookline Hills. After leaving the train, take a right on Cypress Street and walk to Walnut Street. Take a right on Walnut Street to Warren Street. Take a left on Warren Street. Fairsted is on your right. Or take Bus 60 from Kenmore Station to the intersection of Boylston Street (Route 9) and Warren Street. Follow Warren Street one-eighth of a mile to Fairsted.

By car: From Boston or Cambridge, follow Huntington Avenue from Copley Square. At the Jamaicaway overpass, Huntington becomes Boylston Street (Route 9). Continue on Route 9 to the third major intersection (Warren Street). Turn left and follow Warren Street to Fairsted.

From the west, take Exit 20 off I-95 (Route 128) and follow Boylston Street (Route 9) five miles. At the first intersection after the Brookline Reservoir (Warren Street), take a right and follow Warren Street to Fairsted.

From the south, take the Southeast Expressway (I-93) to the Massachusetts Avenue exit. Take a right at the end of the exit and follow Massachusetts Avenue to Huntington Avenue. Take a left on Huntington and follow Huntington to the Jamaicaway overpass, where it becomes Boylston Street (Route 9). Continue on Route 9 to the third major intersection, turn left on Warren Street, and follow the signs to Fairsted.

Free parking is available.

Forest Hills Cemetery

Overshadowed by the older and far more famous Mount Auburn Cemetery in Cambridge, Boston's Forest Hills Cemetery is considered by many to be an even better example of a 19th-century garden cemetery—by no less of an authority than the man who built Mount Auburn itslf.

Horticulturalist Henry A. S. Dearborn laid out the Cambridge precursor in 1831 as America's first country cemetery, spawning copies including Laurel Hill in Philadelphia and Green-Wood in Brooklyn. But when Dearborn went on to be elected mayor of then independent Roxbury in 1847, he wasted little time creating another cemetery that would rival any of those.

The favorite of Boston's wealthiest families, Forest Hills would come to boast one of the nation's finest collections of 19th-century sculptures, including no fewer than six by Daniel Chester French, nestled among its rolling hills, trees, gardens, terraces, and man-made ponds.

But the greatest endorsement of the cemetery was Dearborn's. He had his famous Revolutionary War–hero father and his mother disinterred and taken from Mount Auburn to become the first people laid to rest at Forest Hills.

The Romantic and the Practical

The early 19th century was a philosophical time in this most intellectual of cities. Democracy was new and fragile. Transcendentalists and abolitionists proselytized in public parks. There was also a new romantic idea of death as eternal repose and a movement toward designing peaceful rural cemeteries, starting with the Cimetière du Père-Lachaise in Paris in 1804. This idea was first imported into the United States at Cambridge, in Mount Auburn, which also incorporated the trendy "picturesque" style of English pleasure parks, with rolling hills, ponds, ledges, trees, and shrubs.

By 1847, there were also practical problems to consider. Boston's early burial grounds were becoming so full, graves were being reused, with the dead being laid on top of one another. That year, Dearborn was elected mayor of Roxbury, then a fast-growing suburb where many of the city's richest had their country homes. He immediately bought 72 acres in the Jamaica Plain section from a farmer named Joel Seaverns,

and by June 28, 1848, Forest Hills was consecrated.

This cemetery would be different from Mount Auburn in one important way. It was founded as a public rather than a private cemetery, and was to be nondenominational, with its grave lots reasonably priced—an important gesture to the American democratic ideal. That meant ordinary people could be laid to rest there, not just the rich and famous.

Olmsted's Inspiration

The cemetery is laid out along winding avenues named for trees—White Oak, Red Oak, Willow, Walnut, Cherry, Hemlock, Fir, and Aspen; and with connecting footpaths named for flowers—Rose, Rhododendron, Laurel, Grape, Azalea, Ivy, and Violet. Nearly 30,000 trees were planted or imported, including beech, linden, oriental spruce, Norway spruce, Japanese umbrella pine, and even sequoia. The bucolic wooded cemetery is said to have inspired Frederick Law Olmsted well before he designed Central or Prospect parks in New York or Boston's Emerald Necklace. Smaller crabapple, dogwood, yellowwood, hawthorn, and other trees went up in newer sections opened after landscaping tastes changed. An artificial lake, Lake Hibiscus, was added in 1852.

Roxbury was annexed by Boston in 1868, and the cemetery was taken over by a private organization, the Proprietors of Forest Hills, who bought it from the city for a dollar. It had doubled in size by then, with 9,000 people already interred.

Forest Hills has since grown to 280 acres and, after being plagued by vandalism and neglect, has been largely restored.

Egyptian vs. Gothic

The main approach to Forest Hills Cemetery wasn't always an imposing entryway. The Gothic-style gate that stands today, with its arches and spires of Roxbury puddingstone, replaced an unpopular Egyptian Revival–style portico built by Dearborn, which had the principal effect of leaving visitors confused. Gothic, not Egyptian architecture was most closely associated with religious structures in the 19th century, and the portico was taken down in favor of this replacement Gothic gatehouse almost immediately after the Civil War, in 1865. Next door are the cemetery office and Forsyth Chapel, both in the Gothic

Death and the Sculptor *was created by Daniel Chester French in memory of Martin Milmore and his brother, Joseph. In this bronze memorial, the angel of death takes the hand of a young sculptor as he carves a sphinx from stone.*

fashion and both designed by Henry van Brunt, the architect responsible for Harvard's ultra-Gothic Memorial Hall and the First and Second Church in Boston's Back Bay.

Gravesites as Art

By far the cemetery's finest sculpture sits just inside the main gate to the left, at Tupelo and Greenwood avenues. Called *Death and the Sculptor,* it was designed by Daniel Chester French in memory of Martin Milmore and his brother, Joseph, a stonecarver; they died in 1883 and 1886, respectively. An Irish immigrant, Martin Milmore was a disciple of the sculptor Thomas Ball, creator of the Washington equestrian statue in the Public Garden. After apprenticing with Ball, he would create the Roxbury Soldiers' Monument at this cemetery, the Soldiers and Sailors Monument on Boston Common, and a sphinx at Mount Auburn Cemetery memorializing the Union dead.

The high Corinthian column of white marble, also near the entrance, marks Mount Dearborn, where Dearborn, his father, and other relatives are buried. Atop the next hill, on Mount Warren Avenue, an Egyptian Revival–style obelisk marks the grave of Marshal Pinckney Wilder, who died in 1886. A scientist and amateur horticulturist, he helped found the Massachusetts Institute of Technology and was president of the Massachusetts Horticultural Society. The 1876 bell tower, which stands between here and the entrance gate, once afforded panoramic views but is no longer open to the public; nor is the bell used any more.

Just below here, on Fir Avenue, is a sculpture of a sorrowful young woman in mourning, called *Grief,* a monument to Caroline and George L. Randidge, who died in 1895 and 1890. The statue was created by German-born sculptor Adolph Robert Kraus, the base by architect Carl Fehmer.

Fir Avenue merges into Tupelo, which turns gently into Cedar Avenue, site of another memorial to the Forsyth family: a Renaissance-style bronze-cast female figure that is the only known work in the area of the German-born sculptor Lee Lawrie, designer of the famous statue of Atlas holding up the world at Rockefeller Center in New York.

Paralleling Cedar Avenue is Consecration Avenue, and where that joins Magnolia is the memorial to manufacturer and philanthropist George Robert White, a cemetery trustee who died in 1922. This, too, is the work of Daniel Chester French, which White himself commissioned in 1905, well before his death: a bronze standing angel of peace with clasped hands and huge outstretched wings. Another large angel, also in memory of White, is in the Public Garden.

Near here is a stone footbridge designed by William Preston. It, too, evokes the Public Garden, where Preston designed the footbridge over the lagoon. Across the bridge on the left is an art deco–style memorial to Edward Thaw, Jr., who died piloting his own plane over New Mexico in 1934. The white granite memorial, by the sculptor Gerome Brush, depicts a young man wearing a pilot's scarf being watched over by the archangel Michael, who has one hand on his sword and the other on the young man's shoulder.

Crossing the Lake

The next collection of noteworthy gravesites begins across the lake, near the cemetery's Walk Hill Street Gate. First, on Chestnut Avenue across from Fern Hill, is buried Eugene O'Neill, the temperamental playwright who won an unrivaled four Pulitzers and the Nobel Prize for works including *Long Day's Journey Into Night* and *The Iceman Cometh*.

Chestnut becomes White Oak Avenue, and before the road forks there's a Newfoundland dog carved of red sandstone, lying atop the grave of Henry Bernard, who died in 1853. The extraordinarily lifelike dog was carved by Henry Dexter, who also created the first memorial sculpture at Cambridge's Mount Auburn Cemetery.

Take White Pine Avenue to Hemlock. There, off Cherry Avenue, is the Clark Memorial, also designed by Daniel Chester French, who used his five-year-old daughter, Margaret, as the model for the kneeling angels at each end. Farther along Hemlock on the left is Althea Path, the final resting place of poet and Harvard professor e. e. cummings, who died in 1962. Though Cummings was famous for writing his poems in small letters only, he is memorialized on his grave as EDWARD ESTLIN CUMMINGS, all in upper case.

Soldiers and Abolitionists

Back in the direction of Walk Hill Street is Ageratum Path, where Unitarian minister Edward Everett Hale is buried. Hale, who died in 1909, is famous as the author of "The Man Without a Country." On Smilax Path, which is parallel to Ageratum, is the gravesite of abolitionist William Lloyd Garrison. Garrison, who died in 1879, was the founder of the New England Anti-Slavery Society and editor of the influential antislavery newspaper *The Liberator*. Though the memorial here is simple, there is a statue of Garrison on the Commonwealth Avenue Mall.

Continue down Smilax to Poplar Avenue. There stands the famous Roxbury Soldiers' Monument, called *The Citizen Soldier*, a seven-foot statue of a Union Soldier resting on his rifle and looking sadly toward the graves. Created by Martin Milmore, it was so popular that tiny reproductions were made and widely sold. Thirty-nine soldiers are buried here, including eight killed at Antietem. Among the veterans is Frederick Pyne of the U.S. Colored Troops, who died in 1870.

Also off Poplar Avenue is the Firefighters' Lot, purchased with public donations in 1856. At its center is a 1909 statue of a firefighter in full uniform by Canadian John Albert Wilson.

Follow Poplar toward Lake Hibiscus, and at Rhododendron Path is a sculpture of St. John the Evangelist, created by Thomas Ball in 1873, which marks the gravesite of rags-to-riches music publisher Oliver Ditson who died in 1888. On Rhododendron Path is another Daniel Chester French work, the 1906 Slocum Memorial, a female figure in relief on a stone slab. At Lake Hibiscus, on Fountain Avenue, is the Chadwick Mausoleum, a Gothic Revival–style church-like stone memorial to the Chadwick family, which owned a lead works. Its patri-

The Roxbury Soldiers' Monument, or The Citizen Soldier, was dedicated on May 30, 1868, the first Memorial Day celebrated in the United States.

This nine-foot statue was sculpted by John Albert Wilson and dedicated in 1909. Wilson purportedly used an actual fireman as the model for the work. The Firefighters' Lot, where the monument resides, is rededicated each year on the second Sunday in June with a firemen's parade.

Avenue, Jamaica Plain. Phone: 617-524-0703.

How to Get to the Cemetery

By subway: Take the MBTA Orange Line or Bus 39 from Copley Square to Forest Hills Station. Leave the station through the Hyde Park exit and cross Washington Street to Tower Street. Follow Tower Street one block to the Forest Hills pedestrian gate.

By car: From Boston or Cambridge, take Storrow Drive to the Fenway/Park Drive exit and follow the signs to the Riverway. The Riverway becomes the Jamaica Way and then the Arborway. Where the Arborway intersects with Route 203 East, go straight on Route 203 East past the Arnold Arboretum. Continue another half mile onto an overpass, where the Forest Hills MBTA station will be on your right. At the next rotary, take the first right onto Forest Hills Avenue.

From the west, take Route 128 (I-95) to Route 9 East. Continue on Route 9 for seven miles to the Riverway in Brookline, following the signs toward Dedham and Providence. Follow the signs to the Arnold Arboretum. Continue another half mile onto an overpass, where the Forest Hills MBTA station will be on your right. At the next rotary, take the first right onto Forest Hills Avenue.

From the south, take the Southeast Expressway (I-93) to Exit 11 (Granite Avenue/Ashmont) onto Route 203 West. Travel four miles on Route 203. The cemetery will be on the left.

Parking is available along Forest Hills Avenue.

arch, Joseph Chadwick, who died in 1902, was president of the cemetery's board of trustees.

Back toward Walk Hill Street is Citron Avenue, which runs just inside the Forest Hills perimeter—and is the site of one of its most poignant monuments, the *Boy in the Boat*. It's the grave of 4-year-old Louis E. Mieusset, who died in 1886, and whose mother commissioned this marble statue of her son with one foot in and one foot out of a small skiff. It's now encased in glass to protect the fragile sculpture.

The grand memorials of the Victorian age are unlikely to be carved again, however. Even many of the historic notables of the 19th and 20th centuries chose not to mark their graves with monuments like these. Among the famous also buried here amid the groves, and scenic vistas are John Collins Warren, who performed the first public operation in which ether was used to anesthetize a patient, and who died in 1856; Lewis Edson Waterman, founder of the Waterman Pen Company, who died in 1901; and Louis Prang, the German-born founder of the American greeting card industry, who died in 1909.

Forest Hills Cemetery is open daily from 7:30 a.m. to dusk. The cemetery office is open 8:30 a.m. to 4:30 p.m. There is no admission charge.

The cemetery is at 95 Forest Hills

INDEX

Page numbers in ***boldface italics*** refer to illustrations and maps.

U-V

W-Z